Brazilian Jiu-Jitsu

Black Belt

TECHNIQUES

Brazilian Jiu-Jitsu

Black Belt

TECHNIQUES

Jean Jacques Machado

with

Kid Peligro

Invisible Cities Press
50 State Street
Montpelier, VT 05602
www.invisiblecitiespress.com

Library of Congress Cataloging-in-Publication Data

Machado, Jean Jacques.
Brazilian jiu-jitsu : black belt techniques / Jean Jacques Machado with Kid Peligro.
p. cm.
ISBN 1-931229-32-5
1. Jiu-jitsu—Brazil. 2. Jiu-jitsu—Training. I. Peligro, Kid. II.Title.
GV1114.M337 2003
796.815'0981—dc21
2003012256

Anyone practicing the techniques in this book does so at his or her own risk. The authors and the publisher assume no responsibility for the use or misuse of information contained in this book or for any injuries that may occur as a result of practicing the techniques contained herein. The illustrations and text are for informational purposes only. It is imperative to practice these holds and techniques under the strict supervision of a qualified instructor. Additionally, one should consult a physician before embarking on any demanding physical activity.

Printed in The United States

Second Printing

Book design by Peter Holm, Sterling Hill Productions

For my students, friends, brothers, and especially my wife Jaqueline and daughters Jullie and Camilla, who have been with me and supported me through good times and bad.

Contents

Introduction

Welcome to the world of black belt jiu-jitsu fighting. My world. I have been competing in this world for a long time—my entire adult life, in fact. And I've been training others to compete in this world for almost as long. Along the way I've noticed a few things. Things people do right, and things they do wrong. These observations were part of the reason I wanted to write this book.

One thing I've noticed is that often instruction is too rigid. Students are taught to commit moves to memory and to repeat them the same way every time. You can get by with this at the beginning levels, but by the time you reach the advanced levels—the focus of this book—you will find yourself at a serious disadvantage if your moves don't flex to deal with the dynamics of each individual situation. That's why in this book I've tried to give you lots of options, and encouraged you to think for yourself. Because in the real world things don't always go down like they do in a textbook, and if you are the one who can create on the spur of the moment, you are going to win.

Another thing many people overlook is the fact that jiu-jitsu—almost any martial art, for that matter—happens fast. It is a series of moves, all predicated on what has happened just before, and the most important thing you can learn is to instinctively transition from one move to the next without having to stop and think about it. For that reason, almost all positions I present in this book are sequences of moves that end either with the mount or with a submission. I truly believe this will make you a much better fighter where it really counts—in the ring.

If you know me, then you know that my style is a very distinctive form of jiu-jitsu, based on speed and submissions, not points. People have found that this style lends itself particularly well to no-gi submission wrestling, which tends to be a faster and more aggressive game than traditional jiu-jitsu. If no-gi fighting is your thing, then you won't be disappointed: many of the positions in this book are designed specifically for no-gi fighting, and the vast majority of the rest work equally well for it.

All this makes *Black Belt Techniques* the most useful tool yet for advanced practitioners. My coauthor Kid Peligro and I put a lot into it, and we hope you get just as much out of it.

The Basics

The positions in this book speak for themselves. You should have no trouble following them and incorporating them into your game. But I have seen practitioners—even black belts—with serious basic errors in their technique. To avoid that, it's essential to go over my basic philosophy when it comes to training and instructing, and make sure we're on the same page before we begin.

Finding the Right Approach to Training

It is of utmost importance for you to choose the quality of training that you participate in carefully, not only the school and head instructor but also the training partners and advanced students. You must immerse yourself in an atmosphere of success and absorb that on all levels if you are to become a champion yourself. Of course, the academy has limits of what it can do for you. I can give you all the tools to become a champion, but I can only go so far. You have to *want* to become a champion. You have to train harder than the others, get in better physical condition, and be more dedicated.

You need to train for at least two years, three times a week, before you can say that you really know jiu-jitsu. Until then you are a novice. You may think you know jiu-jitsu, but really you don't. By the time you are an advanced purple belt or a brown belt, you should be showing the influence of my training. The early belts do not have the characteristics of my school.

The instructor is the most important consideration in choosing an academy. I find it very necessary to be the best that I can be and to set an example for others. If I present myself in a good light, my students will admire me and try to be like me, but in their own way—and not just when it comes to jiu-jitsu. They may become a good doctor, or a good engineer, or whatever, but it is my hope that they will do so with the same determination and dedication to the profession that I have shown toward jiu-jitsu.

In the academy there are various different types of students. There are those that love competition and there are others that don't, but train for other reasons, like to lose weight, for exercise and camaraderie, or to develop their character. Jiu-jitsu helps with this because it develops confidence and social skills. I respect everyone's reasons, but I also encourage everyone to help the ones that are going to compete, so that it becomes a group victory when someone from my academy wins.

When I am training with one of my students and I see that he is having difficulty with a certain move or position, first I try to show the proper technique and then, without telling him, I get us into that position countless times so that he can practice over and over the moves I have shown. If he still has problems with it, then I go back and correct him. If he does not, then I simply sharpen his reactions and reflexes so that the move comes out faster and more automatically each time. I do that silently so that he doesn't notice, and also so that he is not always needing my advice or instructions to execute a move, because some day I won't be there to tell him the right thing to do. So my intention as a teacher, especially with advanced students, is to have them be free and confident with their abilities so that they can solve any problem they face.

And the learning goes both ways, no matter how advanced you are.

Jean Jacques secures across-side position on Marcio Cromado, 2000 ADCC.
Marcelo Alonso/O Tatame photo

I learn from my students, too, even the white belts. I learn a lot from beginners because they always bring a fresh way of thinking that expands the sport. Sometimes a new white belt will react differently from all my advanced students to something I throw at him, and that fresh reaction will be something that will add to my game. The beginner is unpredictable; it is usually harder to train with a white belt than it is with a blue belt, because the blue belt reacts the way you expect—the way he was taught—and that makes it easier to anticipate his reactions, while a white belt reacts unpredictably. That is important, because you need to be able to react to whatever comes your way at any time, to become a better black belt and no-rules fighter.

Often, when you train with beginners, they rely on power and strength, rather than strategy, and that is a good challenge for you as well. Your natural reaction may be to try to match the strength, because you either don't know enough or are not used to deflecting the power. It is a measure of progress to train with a person that uses power and be able to go around that power or use that power to your own bene-

Always attacking: Jean Jacques goes for the gold against Caol Uno, 1999 ADCC finals. Susumu Nagao photo

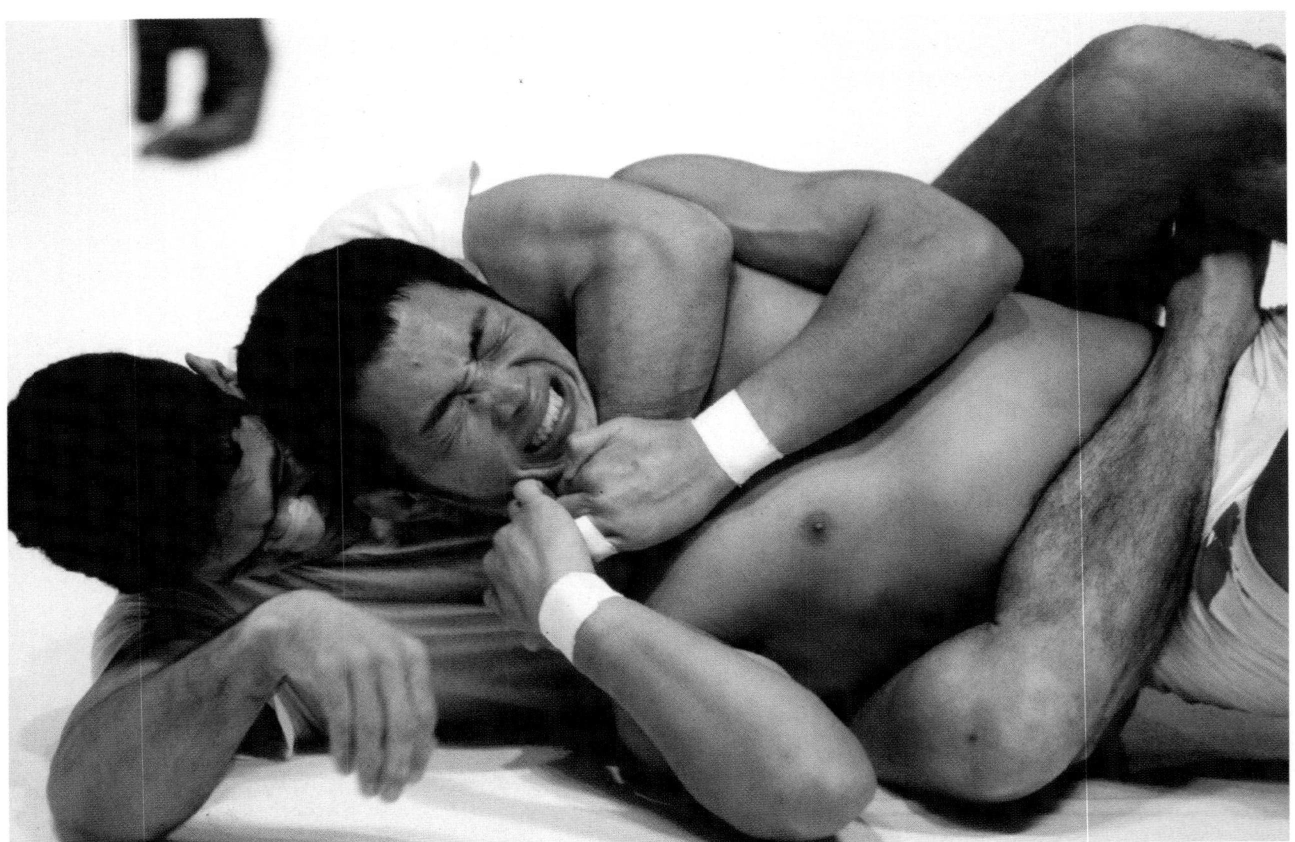

fit. Again, the best way to learn to do this is to train with beginners until you get used to applying your technical skills to deflect their strength away from you.

I always say that it is extremely important to train with a variety of people so that you can develop a complete game. If you constantly train with advanced practitioners, then the game may stalemate, with you each always doing the same thing, and that can stifle progress. Another advantage of training with a beginner is that you can get to the same position frequently and sharpen that position. As you get better and understand the finesse and the nuances of the position, then you should try the same thing with a more advanced fighter, say a blue or purple belt. And once you have that position working with the advanced fighter, then you should try to use it with a brown belt and finally a black belt. If you immediately try to use a new position with a tough black belt, you may never make it work at all. If you are still working on the mechanics of the position, you might be able to use it on a purple belt, but not with a black belt. Additionally, since a black belt has many defenses in his arsenal, you may not be able to return to that position, because you have a lot less control of the direction of the training with an advanced fighter. So you may never get the necessary practice with the position.

It is like trying to do the 110-meter hurdles before you have learned how to walk. It just won't work. First you have to learn how to crawl, then walk, then run, then sprint. Once you have the mechanics of sprinting down, then you can think about going for the hurdles. To get better, you have to go one step at a time.

Developing Your Style

Jiu-jitsu is a personal thing. There are techniques that work well for me, but don't work well for you. There are a great variety of body types out there, and not every position will work for all of them. You can't make an elephant fight like a mouse and you can't make a mouse fight like an elephant! Each person has his own reaction and that is specific to the person. Some are faster, some are slower, some have longer legs, some are stronger, so each must adapt his game to his biotype, physical condition, and way of thinking and reacting to things.

It is important for you to learn the positions and try to adapt them into your own game, but it is also important to realize that some things are not for you. As an instructor, I need to be aware of this and adjust my teaching to each student. I have conducted many tests in my academy where I showed a position to a group and watched who learned it and who didn't. Some people clearly had an easier time with some techniques. I'll sometimes show a position to a group of five students in a group of thirty, knowing that those five will get this position while the rest won't, and then I'll show a different technique to the rest because I know that it is the one better suited for them.

Each student needs to be taught differently, especially in the case of a private lesson. The lesson usually begins after ten minutes of training, because by then I've seen how you react to certain things. Then I can go and advise what is wrong or right and give options and correct details that will improve your game. Then it all clicks and I see your face light up, and that gives me a great deal of satisfaction. It is a difficult job, but I love it.

As an advanced student, you can't simply take a position and expect it to work for you immediately. It may not work for you at all, but it may just take some adjustment and improvisation to merge it with your style. It is important for you to not give up on something because it doesn't work right away, but to be flexible and adapt the technique. As you become more advanced, you need to learn how to adjust the position for yourself, but also how to decide which techniques are better suited for you and which aren't. At times you will learn thirty different things, only to have one or two work in your game. Other times you learn a new position and it takes months before you use it. Suddenly, out of the blue it comes into play and becomes a part of your game. That is why it is important to learn the positions in this book, and then later to go back and review them again. You may find that, when you are in a different place with your game, positions that seemed useless before suddenly click into place.

It is very important that, as you are working with this book, you always analyze your training. Really dissect it and see what you are doing well and what you are struggling with. Then take that and use it however you want. What is presented here is a path, one of many possibilities. I cannot show you every option in one book—jiu-jitsu is ever expanding and there are limitless options—but what I have tried to do here is give you something to think about, some sequences of attacks, so you can expand on them and create your own game and sequences.

Progress is very difficult in jiu-jitsu, because along the way you have so many things to consider. At first you don't know many techniques, but you can concentrate on your opponent's balance and where he has his weight and use that. Later, you learn more techniques, and all of a sudden you start to add them to your game. Now you have to decide quickly which one is the right one for that moment, for the situation that your opponent is presenting to you, and you stop thinking about where their weight is or what they are trying to achieve. After a while, you start putting it all together. It's like driving. After you have mastered it, you do things automatically.

Perfection involves knowledge, timing, and execution. A good instructor can teach you many things, but when the time comes to execute your moves with the necessary speed and precision, that is up to you. Of course, training and repetition help. The more training partners you have the better, since different sizes and shapes and personalities will force you to develop a well-rounded game.

I see the blue belt stage as a sponge. The more you train, the more you learn. Whether you are aware of it or not, your brain is absorbing all the training that you are doing. Sometimes the things you pick up are imperceptible, like the pressure your opponent uses when passing your guard. Even if you don't practice that, you still register it and may come to use it later. The blue belt is the best phase in jiu-jitsu; everything you can absorb then will be good for you. As you begin to progress and change belts to purple, brown, and finally black, you begin to focus. You start to discard the stuff that doesn't work for you and create your own style.

Jean Jacques controls Hayato Sakurai's back, 1999 ADCC semifinals.

Susumu Nagao photo

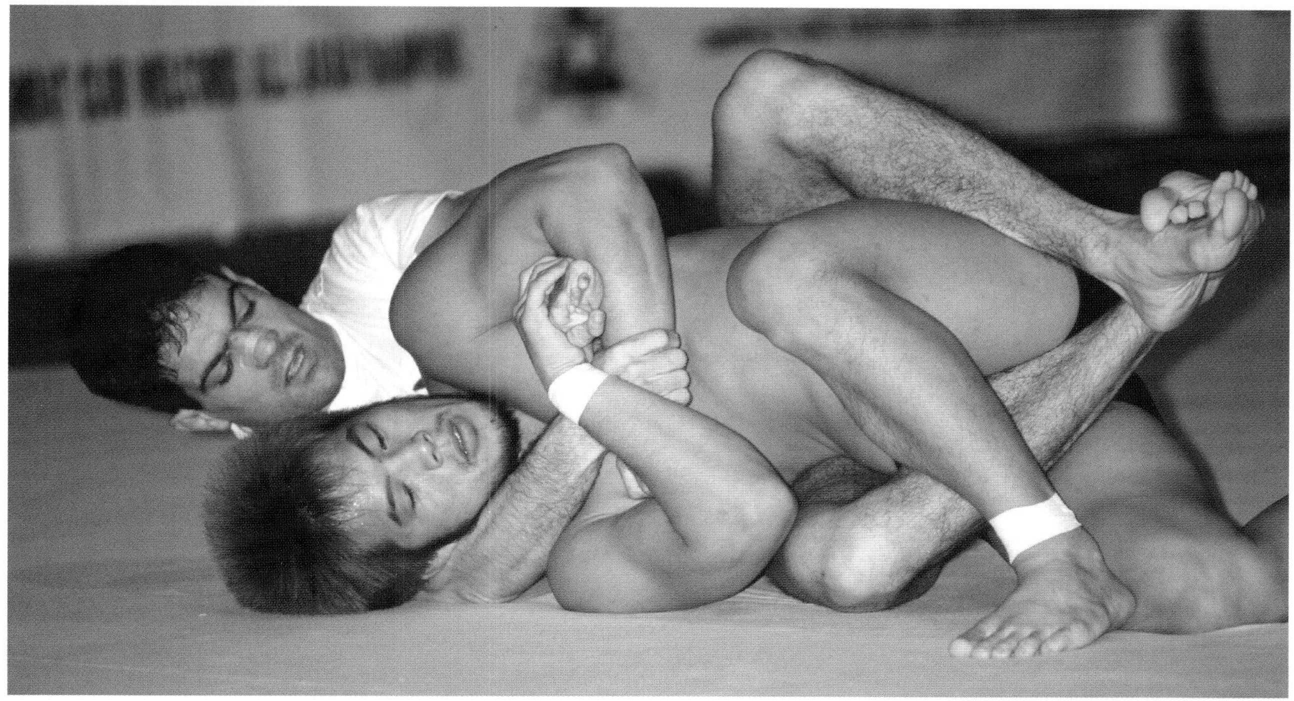

Still, good instruction is essential at every level. A good instructor will give you direction, clarity, and a fresh perspective, because sometimes you can get stuck in a certain problem. If you don't get direction, then it can be frustrating. Many people get stagnated and don't have the right instruction at the right moment to set them free to go forward and create again. To go back to the driving metaphor, sometimes you can take a wrong road that doesn't actually go to your destination. If you don't stop and ask directions, you can travel a long way before you realize your error. That's what I am there for: to flag you down and say, "No, you don't want to go down this road at all. Take that other road instead." And that is what this book is for, too. Not only does it show you some of the fastest roads to take, but also some beautiful shortcuts between the roads that only a few of us locals know about!

One of the roads that people generally miss is the one using their weaker side. There are a few people who are naturally ambidextrous, but most people have a better side. It is very natural while developing your game to have a stronger preference for one side. You feel better attacking from the right or defending the guard on the left. But this can become a trap. There are those who immediately turn to one side to defend the guard and if you attempt to pass on their opposite side, they

1998 Pan-American Jiu-Jitsu Championships.
Marcelo Alonso/O Tatame photo

don't know what to do. In effect they are "blind" on that side. Although that is common it is also a big problem. You may get by like that for a while, but eventually you will be exposed. I even know of top fighters who have only "one eye," but because of the skill and strength they bring to that side, they are able to hide their weaknesses. But sooner or later, they will meet an opponent who has a field day with their weakness.

You should always strive to be equally proficient from both sides. As you learn the positions in this book, make sure you can reverse them all successfully. Of course this doesn't come easy. One way is to practice both sides constantly, until you have perfect execution on both sides. It can be hard to learn this way, however. The more natural way is to master the mechanics on one side until you fully understand what is involved, then start applying what you've learned to the opposite side! It will feel unnatural at first, like trying to hit a baseball from the wrong side of the plate, but to improve the "bad" part of your game you have to suffer. Always in jiu-jitsu, to get better you have to suffer a little and actually get a bit worse before you move forward. You stop using the things that are only somewhat effective but are very comfortable for you, and in the long run this expands your game and makes you a much more complete fighter.

For example, if your opponent defends the side attacks very well, and all you know how to do is side attacks, then you are in trouble. If you try a mount, you force him to defend the mount, and that in turn may give you a chance to submit him from your favorite side attack. But if you just stay in your comfort zone, nothing will happen.

This is why it is important to train with a variety of people. If you always train with the same person, he will start to understand your game and anticipate it, and that will negate your actions. Or, if he is a weak opponent, your moves will work every time, and you won't develop the other options you will need when you fight a better opponent. If you don't have much choice and you have to train with the same person all the time, then you need to create new situations to keep things fresh.

Sometimes you have to give a little bit to gain something else. For instance, if you are across-side and your opponent is just locked up defending, maybe you give him a little space to try to escape, and that will open up something else for you. Don't forget the knee-on-stomach. That position is there to force people to open up. When you apply all that pressure and force, sometimes your opponent will expose an arm or a neck, other times he will give you the mount, but the knee-on-stomach opens a lot of doors. Sometimes I put knee-on-stomach and just study the reactions. I use the knee and he defends this way. I do it again and he does the same thing. The third time I am ready to attack.

The Guard

The guard is the most important position to learn in jiu-jitsu. A jiu-jitsu practitioner will spend most of his time either passing or defending the guard. That is true whether you are a beginner or an advanced practitioner. These days in competition 80 percent of the game is either passing or defending the guard. You may know all the submissions in the world, but if you cannot pass the guard properly, you will probably never get to use them. For these reasons, passing and defending the guard figure prominently in this book.

The proper strategy for passing the guard is that the actual act of passing the guard should be the fourth item you address. First you need to make sure that you have good posture and good balance, and that can only come from developing a good base. Second, you need to make sure you defend your arm, to avoid arm locks. Third, you need to make sure you defend your neck, to avoid chokes. Only after you do all this instinctively should you worry about selecting the best technique to use in relation to your opponent's defense.

Many people do not follow that order. They don't think about base, posture, and defense, and thus give their opponent an opportunity for a sweep or submission. Trying to pass without a good base actually gives the person on the bottom a much higher probability of succeeding in a sweep than the one on top has of passing!

Once you have everything set, the guard pass will come from pairing the right techniques with the opportunities that open up, along with your speed and power. Most of the time the advanced athlete has some favorite positions from which to start the pass. Though I mentioned above that you shouldn't have certain attacks that you lean on too heavily, it is inevitable that you'll have favorites. This is fine, so long as they don't narrow your game too much.

Again, do not start to pass the guard unless everything is in order. If someone reaches your neck with an attack, it is better to take several steps back and defend the attack, rather than to proceed and be submitted. Many people get so locked into their plan that they end up being either swept or submitted with an arm lock or choke. Better to go back to zero and start over than to take a chance and lose it all.

There are many different strategies for passing the guard. They adapt themselves to different body types of both the defender and the attacker. Two big keys are controlling your opponent's hips and staying close to him. It is very difficult to pass the guard when your opponent has the ability to move his hips, since he can continuously adjust his position. Staying close to your opponent in a tight position will not only prevent his hips from moving freely, but also take away space for his legs and knees to come around and block your pass.

To be aggressive and a finisher in the guard, the first step is to develop a combination of positions that create opportunities for a submission. If you are capable of keeping your opponent off balance, then his defense won't be as effective, because he must concentrate on avoiding the sweep or regaining his balance. Keep him guessing. *Misdirection* is a highly underappreciated art in jiu-jitsu. Sometimes attack with a submission attempt so that you can get the sweep, and sometimes attempt a sweep in order to open the door for a submission. Sometimes attack an arm in order to get the other arm, or attack a leg to create an opening for something else. There are limitless combinations of elements that lead to the main objective, which is the submission. Of course, each person also has his or her own temperament. Some are aggressive, some are passive, some are flexible, some like the open guard, some like to hold the arms.

Jean Jacques on someone's back can mean only one thing: submission! Against Sakurai, 1999 ADCC semifinals.

Susumu Nagao photo

Maintaining Position

A classic mistake people make—especially when training from a book such as this—is to stop sparring as soon as a position is achieved. In actual competition, one of the most difficult—and useful—things can be *holding* a position. If every time you achieve a good position your opponent escapes, that is useless. You should concentrate on maintaining your gain before going forward and losing what you have. It is a lot of work to achieve a position. If you mount someone and you can keep him there for an hour, there will be a lot of opportunities to submit him. But if he escapes right away, then it just frustrates you and wears you down.

If you cannot maintain side control, you won't have many opportunities to use those attacks, either. If you cannot keep the mount, then you are limiting yourself to only certain submissions. If you take the back and the opponent escapes quickly, then you have just lost the best position that a jiu-jitsu fighter can get. First learn to maintain the back position, then learn to choke.

Everyone wants to learn to submit. It is a lot more exciting than learning to hold a position. But this is like practicing taking shots on goal in soccer without learning how to dribble. Control is the key. In my acad-

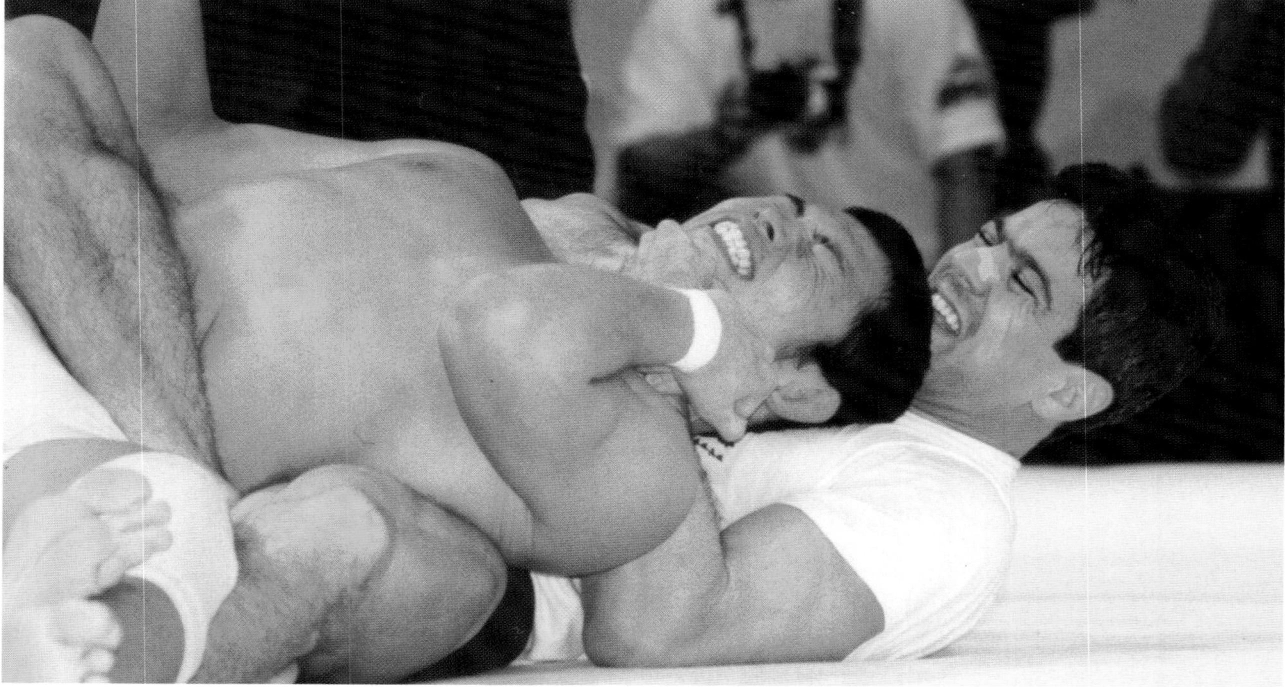

Jean Jacques attacks Caol Uno's neck, 1999 ADCC finals.
Marcelo Alonso/O Tatame photo

emy at one time I noticed that my students were not getting the mount. The mount is perhaps the hardest position to master, because you rarely get there, and it is very hard to maintain. So I did drills specifically for that. I told the students that they couldn't attempt a submission if they weren't mounted on their opponent, so everyone had to try to focus on mounting first, and that helped them a lot. Now everyone loves the mount. Another drill you can do is to start one person mounted on the other. The top person needs to keep the mount and the bottom one needs to escape, no submissions allowed. It is this kind of work, day in and day out, that will pay off in competition.

The Chess Match

A big difference between this book and previous jiu-jitsu books is that this one demonstrates series of moves that lead to a submission, rather than simply showing one move in isolation. I can't overemphasize the importance of this. Martial arts fights are a constant flow of moves and countermoves, each triggered by what your opponent has done. As in a game of chess, you don't simply concentrate on taking one piece; all your moves contribute to an overall plan. An advanced student already has engraved in his mind a set of positions, along with the natural reactions that these positions will induce in his opponent. This is one of the things that separates the advanced belts from the beginners. A black belt will have at least three moves connected and planned out, so that he can be ahead of his opponent.

It is very important to have these sequences down and automatic, not only the initial movement but also the knowledge of the options that your opponent has to react to your attack. This process is acquired with time—time on the mat training, experience, and most important correct instruction and guidance from your teacher. As you advance, you will find that the positions and techniques become second nature to you.

To progress in jiu-jitsu, I tell my students, you are going to learn isolated positions, but every one of them is connected with each other. It is like a puzzle and I put all the parts on the table; your job is to put together the puzzle and make your figure. If I want to sweep the guy, for instance, how do I make him put his weight where I want it to be? I push him one way, he reacts against it, and the end result is his weight is where I want it to be. I push him to the left, he pushes back to the right, and when he does that I sweep him to the right. It is all connected.

I prefer to give my students movement drills, sequences of connected moves. I can get students to do a hundred arm locks in a row in isolation, but when they are training their timing will be wrong if they are not used to doing it in motion. That is something I have done in this book as well. You will find sequences of moves that are tied together by the reaction of the opponent. If you try an arm lock, it is connected to a sweep, a neck choke is connected to the arm lock and the sweep, and so forth. If you do a position, you should stop and analyze the options available to you for each of your opponent's reactions. Start with some of the sequences presented here, but I cannot cover all the options in one book, so be creative; that is what is going to make you progress the most in the sport.

Of course, you can't know exactly how your opponent will react to a particular move. My solution to this has always been to keep firing away with attacks until I get my opponent to react in a way that I can take advantage of. I'm like a machine gun; I shoot a hundred bullets, knowing that at least a few will hit the mark. The other advantage of throwing so many attacks out there is that it gets your opponent out of his comfort zone.

When I fight a large and skilled fighter like Ricardo Arona, for instance, in the finals of the Absolute Division in the 2001 ADCC World Submission Wrestling Championships, no matter what position I find myself in, I must do something to bother him. I need to create a reaction from him! Once I get some kind of reaction, then I can use the patterns that have worked for me before, or use something else that I haven't used but may work against him because of his own reactions. If I pull him, how does he react? If I push him, what does he do? I make a series of continuous actions that lead to a submission. From there I will have to come up with something. I will pull his arm, pull his head, place a hook, hold a wrist, creating a circle of actions that gets faster and faster. Eventually, he gets late in his reaction and I have my opportunity.

Here's a secret: after some time in jiu-jitsu, you end up without the positions. I can't very well explain it, but nowadays I don't practice a specific position in jiu-jitsu. It has all blended into one seamless art for me, as much a part of me as walking. If you see me do a move and ask me why I used it, I can't very well tell you; it's instinctive. If you press my arm in a certain fashion, I'll do one thing; if you press it differently, I'll do something else. I don't have a set game. If you ask me what my favorite position is, I'll say the one that my opponent gives me. My game is sensitive and automatic without being robotic.

Sometimes a student will ask me, "Jean Jacques, I get here and then I get stuck. What do I do?" Then I must put myself in that same position, and I'll give him ten different answers, but if he asks me how it all happened I will tell him that I simply reacted to the situation and all these came out. Every black belt experiences this. At first you learn the principles, and then at some point you just have them inside of you. I can tell when that happens, because I see it in the student as happiness. I see his satisfaction of being able to execute a certain thing or escape from a certain hold.

That is my objective when teaching: to get the student not to become attached to a position or a set of positions, but rather to become reactive to what is happening between him and his opponent. And I don't want you to think of this book like a cookbook. Or, rather, treat it like a master chef treats a cookbook. Do the recipe straight through a few times until you are familiar with it, but after that feel free to play around with it, use it for inspiration, or change some of the ingredients entirely. Just make sure it works in the test kitchen before serving it in

Going for an arm bar against Caol Uno, 1999 ADCC finals.
Susumu Nagao photo

the dining room! The positions in this book are not set in stone; they are set in clay, very soft clay, and you need to mold then to your style and to the situation at hand.

Say you learn a certain half-guard sweep. The hand needs to be here and the foot has to be there, and that may be how it happens in competition, but every time you get to a certain position the situation will be a little different, and you should be able to improvise with the elements that you have and adapt the position to what is happening. Sometimes you get everything right, but more often you need to adapt on the fly.

Becoming a Submissions Specialist

My greatest characteristic is that I am a finisher. To me, submitting an opponent is like a touchdown in football, a knockout in boxing. There is no question about the outcome. It is clear and final. You don't have to rely on judges. With the growth of the sport and the talent increasing, it gets more difficult to achieve submissions, but that is the reason to fight, that is the essence of jiu-jitsu. Jiu-jitsu didn't develop in the tough world of Brazil to win on points; it developed to absolutely defeat your opponent—any opponent.

I try to convey that to my students. I tell them that I'd rather they try to submit their partner than to be thinking about points and winning the round. This may not be the best strategy to winning every competition, but it is the most rewarding way to fight, as well as the only indisputable proof that you are the better fighter. To fight this way, you have to have a lot of movement in your game, changing positions and constantly seeking to improve your position. The movement is what creates openings for the submissions to occur.

I do a lot of specific drills to encourage and sharpen that movement. For instance, I put someone on the bottom and tell them that they have thirty seconds to sweep their opponent, I don't care how. And I tell the person on top that all he needs to do is not to get swept. He isn't trying anything except to avoid the sweep, and that makes it even more difficult for the person on the bottom, but that will force that person to move and attack to achieve the objective. We repeat that for four or five minutes. Sometimes in the middle of a normal training I'll yell, "Thirty seconds to submit your opponent!" That shakes things up, and really reveals who is on top of their game and who isn't. Then we go back to normal training again. I do these things to encourage movement and attacks. My students learn to explode without much preparation. I highly recommend that you try similar drills with your sparring partners.

This may surprise you, but if you want to become a finisher, the most important step is to develop your defense. Once you have a great defense, then nothing that your opponent sends your way bothers you, and you can put all your energy into attacking.

Buddhists say that one of the first steps you need to take to embrace life is to come to terms with your own death. It is the same in jiu-jitsu, only what you have to face is not death but fear of your opponent. Think about a cornered rat. A rat is a frightened animal, but once cornered, it becomes dangerous and formidable and will attack you no matter how big you are. It knows it has nothing to lose, and that knowledge gives it a lot more power than it would normally have. That is how I work with my more passive students. There are those who are very aggressive and will attack all the time anyway, and then there are those who aren't. But once these passive ones master their defense, once they learn they have nothing to lose, then there is nowhere else to go but forward!

No-Gi Submission Wrestling

The rise of events such as the ADCC World Submission Wrestling Championship has made it vital that a fighter learn to compete while not wearing a gi, as well as while wearing one. Fortunately, my game has never been based on using the gi. Because the fingers on my left hand never developed, I couldn't take advantage of gripping the gi. I had to adapt my game in other ways, and that gave me an advantage when everyone began competing without the gi. I didn't have to unlearn the habits that many others did.

A disadvantage can be a gift in disguise. Much as my uncle Helio Gracie was forced to develop new techniques because of his inherent physical disadvantages, and this led to the basic leverage techniques that make jiu-jitsu so effective, so I had to develop new techniques that would work with my disadvantages.

For this reason, most of my positions work both with and without the gi. There are some collar chokes that absolutely need the gi, but otherwise everything is based on speed, surprise, body contact, positioning, and weight distribution to control the opponent.

Because of this, it is *very important* for you to not only follow the written instructions but also closely dissect the photographs and make note of my body positioning and weight distribution in relation to my opponent. This is an extremely important and often overlooked aspect of any instructional book. One can only put so much into words, but absorbing the details of the positioning (if the instructors are qualified masters) will help you get a leg up on the competition.

In truth, I don't see much of a difference between gi and no-gi fighting. The only thing that changes is that, without the gi, the speed of the action increases, since you can't simply hold each other. Submission wrestling allows a greater freedom of movement, and since my game is predicated on movement, it fits my style very well. It is harder for someone to control me and slow my game down—and if you can't slow me down, you're in trouble.

I'm not saying that gi training is not important. It should still be the foundation of anyone's training. And, of course, if you have the gi you should take advantage of it, but you shouldn't be a slave to the cloth. The techniques that I chose for this book are my favorites and are for that reason easily adapted to both situations.

Meet the Authors

Jean Jacques Machado

I was born on February 12, 1968, in Brazil. My mother was the sister of Carlos Gracie Sr.'s last wife, Lair. Aunt Lair and my mother had very strong ties, so they spent a lot of time together and consequently Lair's sons and my brothers and I spent a lot of time together growing up. We got to grow up just soaking in jiu-jitsu. We were like a new clan entering into the Gracie clan life. We started training at a very young age. By the age of twelve or thirteen I started to take the sport very seriously and got involved in competition, as did my brothers Carlos, Roger, Rigan, and Johnny.

You can't imagine the jiu-jitsu atmosphere I grew up in. We would go to the Gracie house in Teresopolis regularly, where my uncles Helio and Carlos and all their children would be running around with us. Some weekends there would be thirty or forty of us, all practicing jiu-jitsu. The Gracies would take a canvas tarp on top of their car to train. Once at the house, that tarp would be stretched out on the lawn and everyone would train together there. We Machados also had a house in the Teresopolis mountains, and we had our own tarp and would train there when we weren't at the Gracie house. So we spent seven days a week training and living jiu-jitsu.

After school we'd go directly to the academy. We would go to Rolls Gracie's Academy in Copacabana. Later, we trained with Carlos Jr. We had to stay through the adult class because Carlos Jr. would take us home at the end of his day. Then the school moved and we would ride the bus for ninety minutes each way to train there. It was a marathon—many times the bus would be full and we had to ride standing the entire way—but we loved to train and wanted to train. Our passion for jiu-jitsu was that strong. As soon as you start to practice jiu-jitsu, then you get the taste and the fever takes over.

Later in life, when I was eighteen or so, I started to train with Rickson Gracie. I don't quite remember how it all started, but Rickson invited me to take privates with him and I couldn't pass that up. He scheduled me at 6:30 A.M. at the Gracie Humaita Academy, so every day, before I'd go to college, I'd wake up at 4:30 so that I could be at the door of Humaita waiting for him. I would spend the morning there and watch him teach his regular privates, and we would train in between each class for a few

minutes, or if someone missed a class then we would train longer. His influence in my jiu-jitsu life was tremendous.

That was a time when my vision into the art expanded, when I first learned to create. I stopped being a repeater of positions and started being an originator. Rickson opened my eyes. Jiu-jitsu is something so personal that it is difficult to teach, but Rickson taught me how to use my body to create. We trained for quite some time, and it only stopped when he left for America. For this reason I believe I have very strong ties with him. Many of the things I do today, I still remember his explanations and his teachings.

I got my black belt when I turned eighteen. By the time I moved to America in 1992, I had won the biggest titles in Brazil and needed new challenges. When I came to America my brothers were teaching in an academy in the Valley that they opened with Chuck Norris, and they were also teaching out of their garage in Redondo Beach. Both academies started to grow, and then they exploded after Royce Gracie's victory in the first Ultimate Fighting Championship in 1993.

Machado schools used to enter the largest number of athletes in every competition and would almost always walk away with the overall team title. We five brothers would combine all our students and enter as one, which made us almost impossible to beat. Today I have my own academy in Tarzana, California, where I train some of the world's top champions. I also train the LAPD and the Navy Seals.

In 1999 I was invited to compete in the pinnacle of submission wrestling events, the ADCC World Submission Wrestling Championships. In my international debut, I submitted all four of my opponents each in five minutes or less, a feat yet to be duplicated. I was runner-up in 2000 and runner-up in the absolute division in 2001, losing by points to an opponent forty-five pounds heavier. Of my eleven wins in my three ADCC events, nine were by submission.

Kid Peligro

I have been involved in the martial arts for most of my life. I attained the rank of brown belt in American kenpo before discovering Brazilian jiu-jitsu. I earned my black belt in that sport after ten years of practice. In that time, I've been fortunate enough to have trained and become friends with some of the best instructors and practitioners in the business, including Rickson, Royler, and Royce Gracie, and, of course, Jean Jacques.

I'm best known as one of the leading writers in martial arts. I'm responsible for regular columns in *Grappling* and *Gracie Magazine*, as well as the most widely read Internet MMA news page, *ADCC News.* I'm also the author or coauthor of three of the most successful martial arts books in recent years: *The Gracie Way, Brazilian Jiu-Jitsu: Theory and Technique,* and *Brazilian Jiu-Jitsu Self-Defense Techniques.*

My broad involvement with jiu-jitsu and MMA events has led me to travel to the four corners of the earth, covering jiu-jitsu, submission wrestling, and MMA events in America, Brazil, Japan, and the Middle East. You might call me an ambassador of jiu-jitsu. In that role, I'm committed to spreading the word about the sport that changed my life.

Pulling guard to arm lock

The best attacks are often surprise ones. One of the best ways to achieve this in jiu-jitsu is to pull guard, making your opponent expect a defensive move, and then turn it into a surprise attack.

1 Jean Jacques stands in base in front of Bryce, holding the gi in a typical way, right hand on Bryce's collar and left holding Bryce's sleeve at the elbow. Bryce uses the same grip. The right hand on the collar by the chest area is very important, as it controls the separation between the two fighters, negating the closeness needed for a throw.

2 In a surprise move, Jean Jacques jumps with both feet on top of Bryce's feet, which prevents Bryce from stepping away.

3 At the same time, Jean Jacques starts to pull Bryce down to the ground, as if he was going to pull guard, by sitting back while keeping his feet on top of Bryce's feet.

4 As his back hits the ground, Jean Jacques is still controlling Bryce's right elbow with his left hand. He opens his legs while pivoting his hips, raising his legs and throwing his left leg over Bryce's head. Notice that Jean Jacques still has his right hand on Bryce's collar and uses it to keep Bryce away, facilitating the arm lock.

5 Jean Jacques then applies pressure by raising his hips while holding Bryce's arm, setting the arm lock.

Passing the guard to arm lock

Jean Jacques is a finisher. He loves shortcuts that lead directly to submissions. In this position, Jean Jacques is attempting to pass the sitting guard and surprise the defender by going straight for an arm lock instead of applying the usual guard-passing technique. Obviously, this is not easily done, or everybody would do it. Surprise is the key; otherwise it is a very easy move to defend and you may end up losing your base. This move is best used during a lull in the battle, when both fighters relax and take a breather. With practice you will be able to sense the proper moment to spring this move.

1 Jean Jacques is attempting to pass the guard. Bryce is sitting down, both feet on the ground, and Jean Jacques is holding both his sleeves. This situation occurs many times in a match, for example if Jean Jacques is using hooks as he attempts to pass.

2 In a surprise move, Jean Jacques pulls Bryce's left arm, lets go of the right arm, and throws his left leg over Bryce's shoulder while he jumps in the air.

3 Jean Jacques lands on the ground with both hands in firm control of Bryce's left arm, and his left leg controlling Bryce's shoulder.

4 Jean Jacques then closes his legs in a figure four, right leg over his left ankle, and pushes Bryce's left arm across his right leg for the arm lock. Alternatively, he can apply pressure to the neck with his hips for a triangle choke.

Passing the guard to a figure-four foot lock

Surprising your opponent by going for a submission while passing the guard yields a variety of potential submissions: the arm lock demonstrated in position 2, or the foot lock shown here. Knowing both options means you can keep your opponent guessing until it is too late. In this case, Jean Jacques is attempting to pass the guard on his knees while his opponent is using the sitting guard. As he is already controlling his opponent's left leg with his right hand, Jean Jacques is half set for this attack already, so it is the better choice.

1 Jean Jacques attempts to pass the guard. In order for the submission to work, his first move is to trap Bryce's right leg with the crease of his left leg.

Detail

Notice in this opposite view how Jean Jacques uses his left leg to trap Bryce's right leg. Jean Jacques will use that hook to help sweep Bryce.

2 Jean Jacques turns to his right and grabs Bryce's left foot with his right hand. At the same time, he uses his left leg to sweep Bryce, lifting it as he goes in a somersault motion over his left shoulder.

3 Jean Jacques continues to roll over his left shoulder. He pushes off his right foot as he pulls Bryce over with his left leg hook.

4 As he finishes the rotation, Jean Jacques wraps Bryce's left foot with his left arm and locks a figure-four grip by holding his right wrist with his left hand. He then applies pressure by pulling Bryce's toes down with his right hand for the submission. Notice that Jean Jacques keeps his legs over Bryce's right leg to prevent the space needed for a possible escape from opening up.

Passing the open guard 1: hand plant

The danger of attacking someone in the open guard is that your opponent has many opportunities to attempt a sweep or a variety of other attacks. That is what happens here: Jean Jacques attempts to pass, but his opponent pivots his hips and blocks the pass by placing his right knee on Jean Jacques's hip, while at the same time keeping his left leg low around Jean Jacques's right foot, setting up a possible sweep. Jean Jacques uses a clever countermove to pass the guard by controlling his opponent's legs and hips.

1 Jean Jacques stands in Bryce's open guard. Bryce has his right knee on Jean Jacques's hips.

2 Since there are many options of attack, Jean Jacques proceeds with caution. He steps right with his right foot, shoots his left hand between Bryce's legs, just behind the right knee, and grabs Bryce's left knee by the gi pants. By stepping right, Jean Jacques neutralizes the possible sweep, while his left hand controls Bryce's hips, preventing any possible attack.

3 Jean Jacques kneels down with his left leg and starts to lower his right knee to the ground, while still using his right foot to hook Bryce's left leg. Notice that he is still using his left hand to hold Bryce's left knee.

4 In firm control of the position, Jean Jacques opens his right arm as he rests his torso over Bryce's right leg and places his left leg against Bryce's butt, locking Bryce's right foot and completely trapping him.

5 Keeping his right arm straight, Jean Jacques switches hooks on Bryce's left leg from his right foot to his left foot. When switching hooks, be sure to have the new hook in place before you release the old hook, otherwise your opponent may trap your left leg and put you in the half guard.

6 Jean Jacques completes the pass by releasing his left foot and stretching Bryce out with his right hand by pulling Bryce's left arm, while his left hand pulls down on Bryce's left knee.

Passing the open guard 2: rolling and taking the back

Another option when confronted with the open guard is to roll the opponent over your head and take his back. This option can effectively deal with an opponent who is flexible enough to constantly readjust his hooks and use his legs well in the open guard. There are two great advantages to this pass: first, you eliminate any chance of a submission; second, you end up in one of the most advantageous positions—on your opponent's back.

1 Jean Jacques stands in Bryce's open guard. In this instance, he waits for a moment when Bryce is adjusting his legs and one of his hooks is not on, though the pass can be used even when the opponent's hooks are in place.

2 Jean Jacques presses his left knee forward into Bryce's right thigh and his left hand presses down on Bryce's chest. At the same time, Jean Jacques uses his left forearm and elbow to prevent Bryce from placing his left foot on Jean Jacques's hips to block his progress.

3 Jean Jacques uses his right hand to grab Bryce's belt while still pressing down on his chest and right thigh.

4 Jean Jacques rolls Bryce over his head by pulling on Bryce's belt.

5 Notice that the choice of hand holding the belt will dictate which way Jean Jacques circles to take the back. In this case he will circle to his left because he is holding the belt with his right hand. If he tried circling to the right he would twist his own wrist.

6 Having reached the back of Bryce, Jean Jacques firmly holds the belt with both hands and sits on Bryce's back.

7 Pushing off his feet, Jean Jacques lifts and pulls Bryce back.

8 Jean Jacques creates the space necessary to place his hooks and take Bryce's back.

Passing the open guard 3: shin block to arm lock

This time Jean Jacques is attempting to pass his opponent's open guard but has disengaged from the opponent's legs. Your opponent will usually circle his feet in this situation, to block any attempt to control his legs. Jean Jacques takes advantage of this moment to use a clever pass to an arm lock.

1 Bryce circles his legs to keep Jean Jacques from holding them and gaining control.

2 In a sudden motion, Jean Jacques uses his right hand to deflect Bryce's left leg. Ideally, you can grab both feet and push them aside, but many times you'll have to be satisfied with just one.

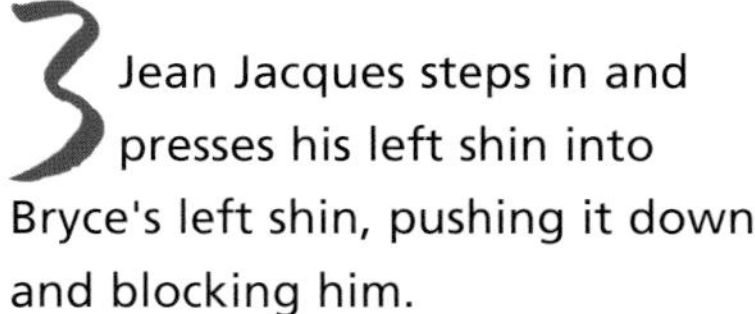

3 Jean Jacques steps in and presses his left shin into Bryce's left shin, pushing it down and blocking him.

4 Jean Jacques pushes off his right leg and continues to apply pressure to Bryce's shin with his own shin. He uses both hands on Bryce's knee to prevent Bryce from regaining position with his legs.

5 Jean Jacques continues to apply pressure with his shin and slides his knee over Bryce's left leg onto his stomach, using his right hand to pull Bryce's left arm.

6 Jean Jacques passes his right leg over Bryce's head and sits back.

7 Jean Jacques completes the arm lock. Notice that he keeps his knees close together to deny Bryce any space for a possible escape. He also controls Bryce's wrist so that Bryce cannot spin his arm to relieve the pressure on his elbow.

Passing the open guard 4: star pass

An acrobatic way to pass the open guard is the star pass. This not only surprises your opponent but leaves you in a very advantageous position, behind your opponent with the possibility of taking his back. This technique, however, requires you to make a complete cartwheel, so make sure you practice the move alone prior to attempting it against an opponent.

1 Jean Jacques is attempting to pass Bryce's open guard. In this case, Bryce does not have any grip on Jean Jacques, but his right knee is up.

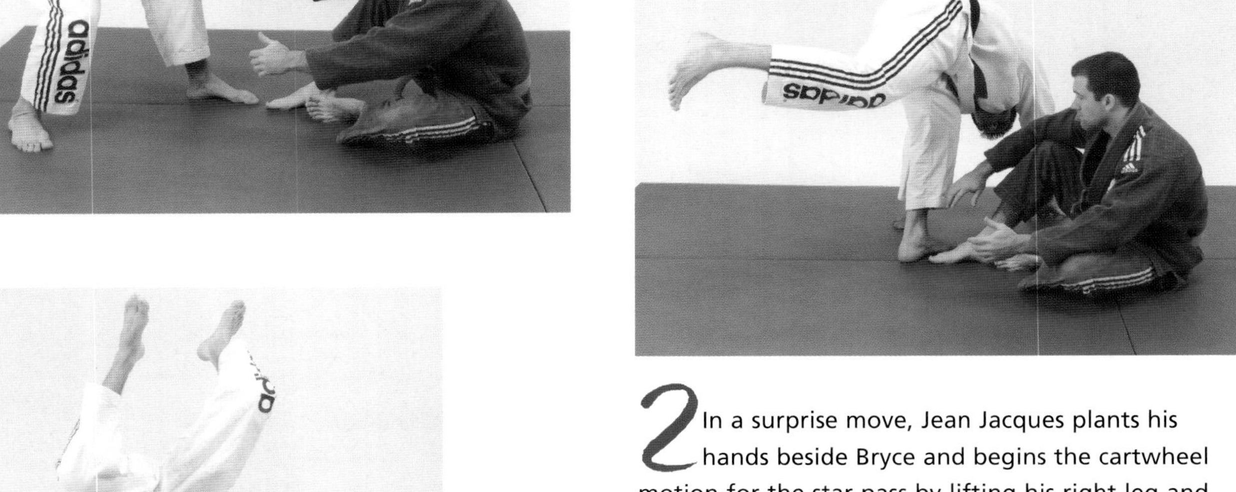

2 In a surprise move, Jean Jacques plants his hands beside Bryce and begins the cartwheel motion for the star pass by lifting his right leg and putting his weight on his hands.

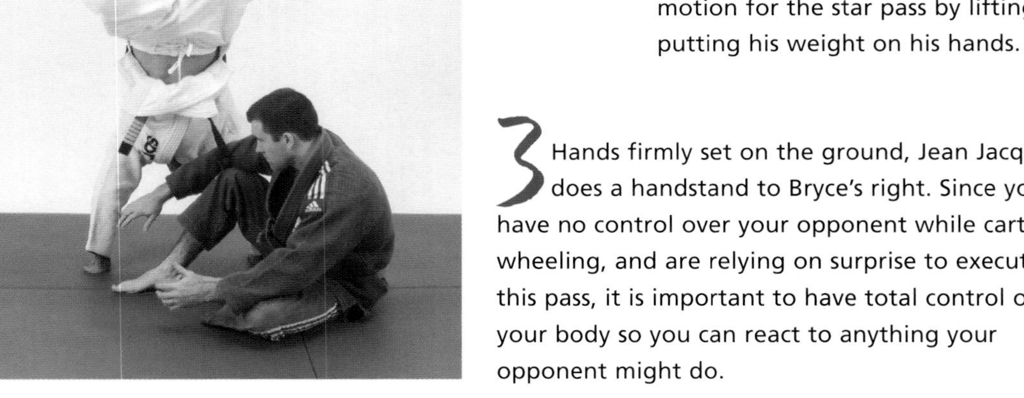

3 Hands firmly set on the ground, Jean Jacques does a handstand to Bryce's right. Since you have no control over your opponent while cartwheeling, and are relying on surprise to execute this pass, it is important to have total control over your body so you can react to anything your opponent might do.

4 Jean Jacques continues the cartwheel, landing with his right leg next to Bryce's right hip.

5 As his other leg lands next to Bryce's left hip, Jean Jacques places his right hand under Bryce's right knee and holds Bryce's left shoulder with his left hand.

6 Jean Jacques finishes by pulling Bryce down with his left hand. He helps the motion by lifting Bryce's right leg with his right hand at the same time. From here, Jean Jacques could quickly capitalize on his position by attacking Bryce's neck with his left hand.

Passing the spider guard 1: circling the hands

The spider guard can give fits to even the most experienced guard-passer. Your opponent has control of both sleeves and presses his feet onto your biceps, often changing the angle of his hips and the pressure against your arms to create instability and open various options for sweeps and submission attacks. Here, Jean Jacques demonstrates a quick and effective way to deal with the spider guard.

1 Bryce has Jean Jacques in his spider guard. He controls both sleeves and presses his feet onto Jean Jacques's biceps.

2 Jean Jacques circles his right hand around Bryce's calf and flicks his elbow up to deflect Bryce's left leg. He uses his left hand to grip Bryce's pants and push Bryce's right leg away.

3 Jean Jacques continues his body's twisting motion, further moving Bryce's legs out of the way. Notice how Jean Jacques uses his right forearm to drive down Bryce's left leg.

4 After clearing all obstacles out of the way, Jean Jacques drops down and lands across-side on Bryce.

5 Jean Jacques completes the across-side position by passing his right arm around Bryce's neck and clamping his chest over Bryce's chest.

Passing the spider guard 2: twist pass

While it is true that spider guards present all sorts of difficulties for the attacker, they also have a weakness—the fact that both your opponent's arms and legs are tied up controlling your arms. This weakness can be exploited, as Jean Jacques does here.

1 Bryce has Jean Jacques in the spider guard.

2 Jean Jacques steps back, lifting Bryce's back from the ground.

3 Jean Jacques twists his arms as if he was turning a wheel, breaking the pressure of Bryce's feet on his biceps.

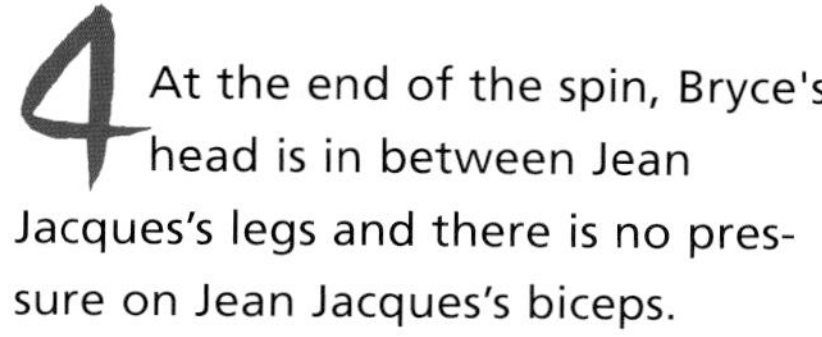

4 At the end of the spin, Bryce's head is in between Jean Jacques's legs and there is no pressure on Jean Jacques's biceps.

5 Jean Jacques thrusts his hips forward and kneels on top of Bryce's head. The force of his hips pushing into Bryce's arms will force Bryce to release the grip on Jean Jacques's arms.

6 Jean Jacques completes the pass by getting across-side position.

Passing the spider guard 3: rollover pass

When the defender has his legs almost perpendicular to the ground and his feet pointing up, the rollover pass works beautifully against the spider guard.

1 Jean Jacques stands in Bryce's spider guard.

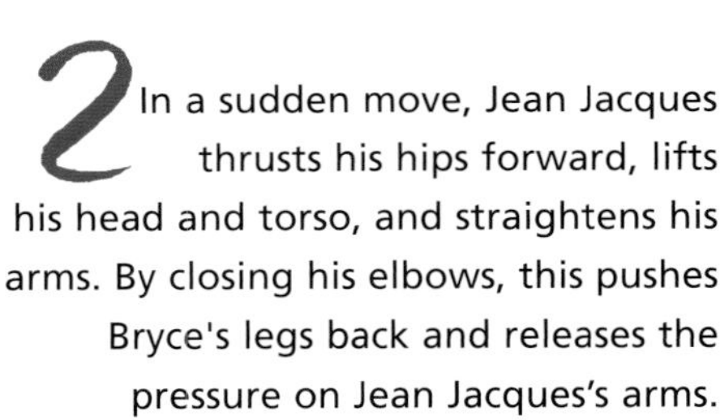

2 In a sudden move, Jean Jacques thrusts his hips forward, lifts his head and torso, and straightens his arms. By closing his elbows, this pushes Bryce's legs back and releases the pressure on Jean Jacques's arms.

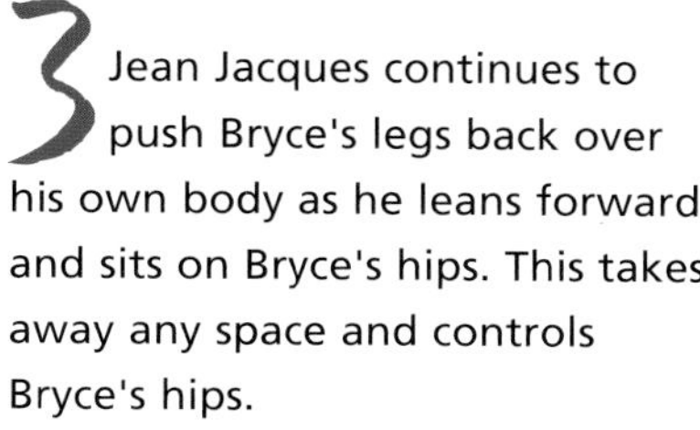

3 Jean Jacques continues to push Bryce's legs back over his own body as he leans forward and sits on Bryce's hips. This takes away any space and controls Bryce's hips.

4 While still sitting on Bryce, Jean Jacques pushes Bryce's legs aside and switches grip with his left hand from Bryce's right leg to his left. He begins to push Bryce's legs to the left side. It is extremely important to maintain close contact with your opponent at this point by keeping your hips on him and holding the leg, otherwise he will be able to scoot his hips away and replace the guard.

5 Jean Jacques completes the pass and takes across-side position.

Passing the spider guard 4: leg spin pass

Another very effective way to pass the spider guard is shown here. This technique helps you control your opponent's hip by using your body weight.

1 Jean Jacques is in Bryce's spider guard.

2 Jean Jacques leans to his left and pushes Bryce's legs toward his left to set up the leg spin pass.

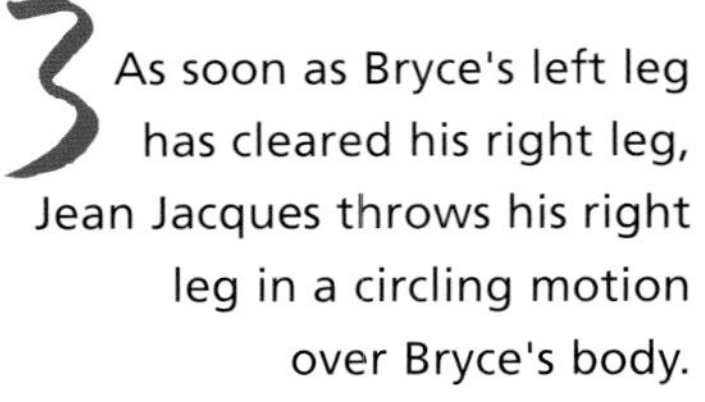

3 As soon as Bryce's left leg has cleared his right leg, Jean Jacques throws his right leg in a circling motion over Bryce's body.

4 Jean Jacques sits on Bryce's legs near the knees while holding them.

Detail
Notice that Jean Jacques is still holding Bryce's legs for absolute control.

5 Jean Jacques lets go of Bryce's legs and slides his body down toward Bryce's side, ensuring that he maintains his weight on Bryce at all times.

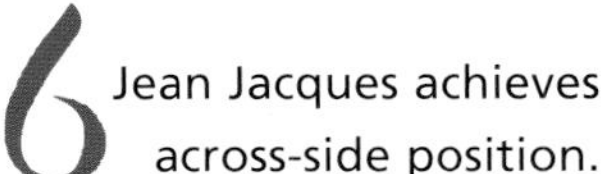

6 Jean Jacques achieves across-side position.

Passing the guard: pass-to-mount variation

In this technique, Jean Jacques uses the traditional guard pass, pulling his opponent's collar, then switches to a more advanced pass-to-mount option when his opponent uses a stiff right arm to block Jean Jacques's left hip.

1 Jean Jacques is passing the guard in the traditional way, his left hand holding Bryce's left collar and his right hand holding Bryce's left leg. In the normal pass, Jean Jacques would use his weight to push Bryce's leg toward his own head, and might also use his right arm to pull Bryce's collar to add pressure to the pass. In this case, Bryce blocks the pass by using a stiff-arm against Jean Jacques's left hip.

2 Jean Jacques switches his hips by bending his left knee while still pushing off his right leg. The hip switch deflects Bryce's stiff-arm, causing it to give. Notice that Jean Jacques sits on Bryce's arm and body to maintain control of the position.

3 Jean Jacques places his left hand on the floor next to Bryce's left hip and pivots over Bryce's head, leading with his right leg. Notice that Jean Jacques has his right leg bent in preparation for step 4.

4 Jean Jacques kneels with his right knee next to Bryce's left shoulder and places his right hand next to Bryce's face to block Bryce's head from moving. This last detail is very important; otherwise your opponent can escape the mount by going between your legs.

5 Jean Jacques completes the position by hooking his right foot under Bryce's arm as he cinches his right arm and shoulder around Bryce's head for maximum control.

Passing the guard to arm lock 2

In this technique, Jean Jacques goes directly from a guard-pass attempt to an arm lock. He starts with the traditional guard pass, but instead of reaching across and grabbing the opponent's collar with his right hand, he holds the opponent's left sleeve instead. Once he has this control, he goes for the submission instead of the pass.

1 Jean Jacques is attempting to pass Adam's guard in the traditional way. This time, however, he switches to grabbing Adam's left sleeve, instead of his collar, so he can set up the arm lock.

2 Jean Jacques takes a step forward with his right leg and lifts his right arm up, pulling Adam toward him.

3 Jean Jacques slides his left knee into Adam's armpit while still maintaining control over his left arm.

4 Jean Jacques throws his right leg over Adam's head to secure the arm lock.

5 Jean Jacques applies pressure to Adam's elbow by lifting his hips. Notice Jean Jacques's proper form, knees together to minimize any space for an escape and both hands grasping the opponent's wrist and hand, thumb pointing up. By controlling the thumb, Jean Jacques eliminates Adam's ability to twist his arm and relieve the pressure to the joint.

Butterfly guard spin pass

In the butterfly guard, your opponent sits up with both feet inside your legs and holds one or both of your sleeves, or one sleeve and your belt. From there he can sweep you or slip to your back. Here, Jean Jacques demonstrates one of the most effective and widely used passes for the butterfly guard.

1 Jean Jacques is in Adam's butterfly guard. Since Adam is holding Jean Jacques's belt with his left hand, Jean Jacques uses his right hand to grab Adam's gi on the left shoulder while at the same time using his left hand to hold Adam's right ankle.

2 Jean Jacques starts the pass by spinning Adam toward his right (Adam's left hand gripping Jean Jacques's belt will prevent him from going the other way) by pulling down on Adam's shoulder with his right hand and lifting Adam's right leg with his left hand. Jean Jacques also turns his hips, kicks his left leg out, and lowers his torso to the ground toward his right shoulder.

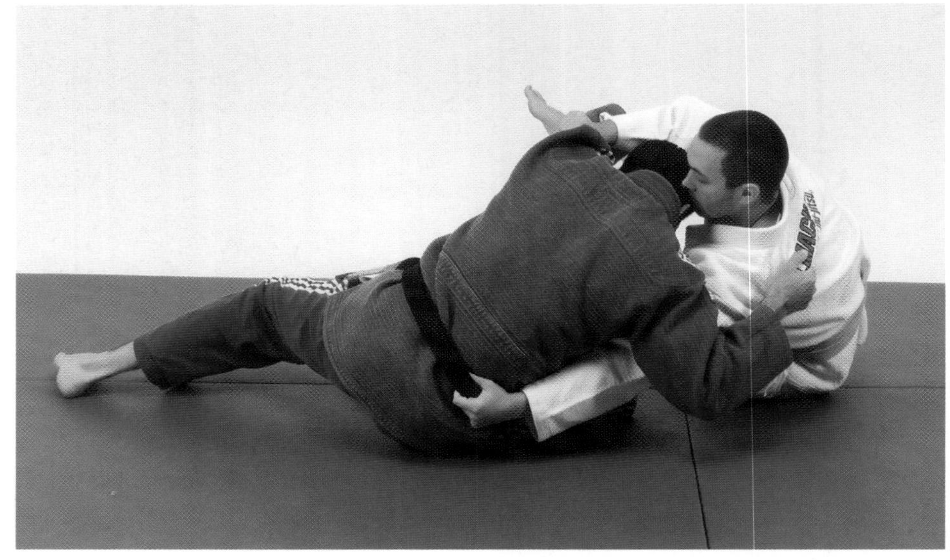

3 Jean Jacques locks his arms around Kid's legs, high on the thigh area close to the hips.

4 By pushing his hips forward, Jean Jacques applies a great amount of pressure to Kid's legs, causing him to open them. In this case, however, Jean Jacques adds a new twist as he closes his legs in a figure-four, right calf behind Kid's right calf, locking his right foot behind his own left knee. When Jean Jacques stretches his body, his hips will push down on Kid's knee while his calf will pull Kid's calf up, causing the knee bar.

TOP LEFT: With Chuck Norris *(left to right):* Jean Jacques (sitting), Rigan Machado, Chuck Norris, and Carlos Machado. **TOP RIGHT:** With Steven Segal *(left to right):* Rigan Machado, Jean Jacques, John Machado, Steven Segal, Carlos Machado, and Roger Machado. **MIDDLE:** Jullie, Jean Jacques, and Jacqueline Machado. **MIDDLE RIGHT:** Jean Jacques and actor Jason Patrick of *Speed 2.*

3 Jean Jacques continues the rotation until he is perpendicular to Adam. Notice that he hasn't let go of his grips and will only do so when he squares his hips.

4 Jean Jacques switches his hips and controls Adam in the across-side position.

Across-side to triangle choke

Submissions are the name of the game in Jean Jacques's style of jiu-jitsu; why mess around with points when you can end the match right away? A good way to achieve this is to trick your opponent into setting up the wrong move. Here, Jean Jacques baits his opponent with a reversal escape, only to surprise him with a triangle choke.

1 Jean Jacques is across-side on Adam, and Adam has his right forearm pushing on Jean Jacques to create space for an escape.

2 Jean Jacques gives space by raising his upper body as he grabs Adam's right gi sleeve near the wrist and pulls it toward him.

3 Feeling the space, Adam turns into Jean Jacques for a reversal, and Jean Jacques allows Adam to come over. With his left hand, he pushes Adam's right arm down, throws his left leg out and over it, and leaves his right knee flat on the ground. Jean Jacques uses his right hand to keep Adam's head close to his body to facilitate the triangle choke setup.

4 As his back reaches the ground, Jean Jacques already has Adam in the early stages of the triangle choke. Jean Jacques's left leg is pressing down on Adam's shoulder, keeping him from escaping, while his right leg completely traps Adam's body with the left arm inside.

5 Jean Jacques locks the triangle choke by locking his right knee over his left foot. He also uses his right arm to push Adam's left elbow across his body to improve the choke.

6 Jean Jacques applies the choking pressure by pulling down on Adam's head and lifts his hips, squeezing Adam's neck and arm.

Across-side to arm lock 1

In this technique, Jean Jacques feigns with a knee-on-stomach position to set up an arm lock. This attack works well any time your opponent has his left arm between your right arm and leg. If his left arm is in another position, you must use another attack.

1 Jean Jacques is across-side and slides his left knee onto Adam's stomach. As Adam starts to move his right arm to block the knee, Jean Jacques uses his left hand to hold Adam's right wrist and press it against his chest. Notice that Jean Jacques has his right arm wrapped around Adam's head with his hand holding Adam's right shoulder. This grip ensures control of Adam's head.

2 Jean Jacques swings his left leg over the trapped arm.

3 Jean Jacques locks it, his right hand holding his left shin. At this point, Adam's right arm is trapped by Jean Jacques's armpit.

4 Jean Jacques braces off his left hand and lifts his hips so he can swing his right leg over Adam's head. Notice Jean Jacques's right hand gripping Adam's left elbow, not allowing Adam to coil his arm back and escape the submission. His left leg traps Adam's head, taking away any space for an escape.

5 Jean Jacques passes his right leg over Adam's head and applies pressure with his hips to Adam's elbow by extending his body.

Across-side to arm lock 2

Position 16 demonstrated an attack when your opponent's arm is trapped between your right arm and leg. Sometimes when across-side, however, your opponent will have his arm close to you on the opposite side, between your left leg and arm. In that case a slight variation of the attack will yield the same result: an arm-lock submission.

1 Jean Jacques is across-side and Adam has an arm between Jean Jacques's left arm and leg.

2 Jean Jacques shifts his body to the left and traps Adam's arm.

3 Jean Jacques extends his right leg and uses his left arm to trap Adam's arm. He uses his right hand to push down on Adam's torso so he doesn't sit up.

Detail

This reverse photo shows how Jean Jacques places his left elbow to trap Adam's arm.

4 Keeping the right arm still, Jean Jacques passes his right leg over Adam's head.

5 Jean Jacques further adjusts the position by sitting back and pulling his left knee with both hands to tighten the lock.

6 Jean Jacques leans back with his torso, applying pressure on the elbow for the submission.

Across-side to arm lock 3: opponent turns

Often times when you are across-side, your opponent will escape by turning into you and holding your leg. If he secures that position and you don't react quickly, he will have a variety of options—none of which are good for you—such as continuing to your back or pulling you down.

1 Jean Jacques is across-side on Adam.

2 Adam starts to turn into Jean Jacques and begins his escape.

3 Adam grabs Jean Jacques's right leg.

4 Anticipating that Adam wants to lock his arms around his thigh, Jean Jacques starts to move before Adam has full grasp of the leg. Pushing off his arms, Jean Jacques throws his body to the left over Adam. Notice that Jean Jacques keeps his right leg on the ground, trapping Adam's arm.

5 As he gets to the opposite side, Jean Jacques is in position for the arm lock: right hand on the ground for balance (in case Adam tries to bridge toward the right), left hand holding Adam's elbow and feet on the ground.

6 Jean Jacques extends his body as he finishes the arm lock.

Across-side to Omoplata

In position 18, Jean Jacques used an arm lock from across-side as his opponent started to escape. In this variation, the opponent gets ahead of Jean Jacques and locks a grip around his leg with both hands. In this case, it will be much tougher to get the arm bar, as your opponent's arms are locked around your thigh. Instead, Jean Jacques prefers to go to the Omoplata, or shoulder lock.

1 Adam quickly turns into Jean Jacques and grabs his leg as he escapes from the across-side position.

2 Jean Jacques pushes off his left leg and arm and rolls over his right shoulder. It is important to keep your right leg tight around your opponent's arm so he doesn't pull it out as you roll.

3 As he continues to roll, Jean Jacques uses his left hand to grip Adam's left elbow.

4 Jean Jacques crosses his legs in a figure-four, locking Adam's left arm in place for the Omoplata. Notice that Jean Jacques uses his right hand to hold Adam's belt so that Adam can't roll over his head and escape the position. From here, Jean Jacques can go to the traditional Omoplata or pull Adam's arm toward his thigh to apply pressure on the elbow joint.

Key lock attack

The key lock, or paintbrush lock, is a common attack from across-side. Your opponent will often have his arms bent at the elbow with his hands protecting his neck from a possible choke, or he may be ready to use them to push you off his chest. In the normal key-lock attack, Jean Jacques would simply use his right hand to push down on his opponent's right wrist, but in this case his opponent reacts and defends by holding Jean Jacques's right arm with his left hand.

1 Jean Jacques attacks Adam's right arm for the key lock. He uses his right hand to push down on Adam's right wrist.

2 Adam blocks the attack with his left hand by either holding Jean Jacques's right arm or by pushing it up away from the floor.

3 Jean Jacques quickly moves his right arm back and lifts his right leg.

4 Jean Jacques traps Adam's arm with his right leg.

5 With Adam's left arm trapped, Jean Jacques goes back to the key-lock attack and pushes down on Adam's right wrist with his hand. This time Adam does not have an arm free to defend the move.

6 Jean Jacques finishes the lock by wrapping his left arm under Adam's arm and locking Adam's hand on to his own right hand. He will apply pressure to Adam's shoulder joint by raising his left elbow while keeping Adam's right wrist on the ground.

Collar and leg choke from across-side

Many times an advanced Brazilian jiu-jitsu fighter will allow his opponent some space for a possible escape as a setup for a submission. In this case, Jean Jacques chooses to allow his opponent to turn into him as he prepares a collar and leg choke. If executed properly, the feint and the attack will surprise even a seasoned martial artist. The secrets to this position are (1) to have a light, loose grip on the collar so as not to attract attention to it (if you grab the collar too hard or tight, not only will you signal your intention, but you will also block your opponent's face, taking away his "escape" route); and (2) to make sure that you don't allow so much space that your opponent senses the alternative attack. Make him struggle to turn into you, and he may not notice the choking hand on his collar until it is too late.

1 Jean Jacques is across-side with his right hand on Adam's collar and his hips switched, left leg on the ground and right leg up.

2 Jean Jacques allows space between his chest and Adam's chest and maintains a loose and light grip on Adam's collar, causing Adam to turn into him for the escape.

3 As Adam turns sideways, Jean Jacques steps back with his right leg and straightens his right arm enough to block Adam's face. He uses the pressure of his chest on Adam's chest to stop Adam from turning too much.

4 Jean Jacques throws his right leg over Adam's head until his foot touches the ground.

5 Once that is achieved, Jean Jacques applies the choking pressure by straightening his right arm as he pulls Adam's collar, closing the gap against his right leg. If he needs more pressure, Jean Jacques will straighten his body and right leg.

Across-side to arm lock 4: collar-choke fake

When you fight more advanced opponents, you cannot take the direct route to a submission; they have plenty of defenses in their arsenals for that. It is important to work things in combination to distract your opponent. Generally, the higher the level of the opposition, the more cunning you will have to be to catch them. In this case, Jean Jacques feigns a downward collar choke to lure his opponent into exposing himself to an arm lock. Note that your initial attack must be solid enough to cause a submission if not properly defended. If the initial attack is half-hearted, a cagey opponent won't need to go to his defense.

1 Jean Jacques starts from across-side with his hips switched, left leg on the ground and right leg up, his right hand on Adam's right collar. He keeps the weight of his torso on Adam's chest. Jean Jacques begins to drive his right elbow to the ground and his forearm across Adam's throat, choking him.

2 Adam blocks the attack by pushing Jean Jacques's elbow up with his left hand.

3 Jean Jacques slides his left knee onto Adam's stomach as he leans over with his body. Notice that at this point Jean Jacques is bracing with his left elbow as he lifts his hips off the ground. This will make it easier for him to execute the next steps.

4 Jean Jacques starts to lean back with his upper body as he pulls back on his right arm, carrying Adam's hand along with it, and slides his left knee further up on Adam's chest. Notice that Jean Jacques has his left shin next to Adam's armpit as he hooks his foot around Adam's left shoulder, blocking Adam's arm from escaping.

5 Jean Jacques holds Adam's left forearm with his right hand and passes his right leg over Adam's head.

6 Jean Jacques falls to the ground for the arm lock. Once again note Jean Jacques's perfect arm-lock execution, knees together, right foot on the ground blocking Adam's face. He controls Adam's wrist with both hands, not allowing Adam to spin or twist his arm to relieve the pressure on the elbow.

Across-side to cross-collar choke

A great attack from the across-side position is the cross-collar choke. This is another example where cunning is useful to achieve the submission. The secret to this position is once again not to telegraph what you want. Allow your opponent space to turn into you for his "escape" as you bait him to the collar choke. A light hold on the collar will camouflage your ultimate intentions.

1 Jean Jacques starts from across-side, hips switched, and grabs Adam's left collar with his right hand. Notice Jean Jacques's left hand holding Adam's right shoulder. He also doesn't apply strong pressure to Adam's chest but rather baits Adam in with a "loose" pressure, his left shoulder up and head back.

2 Sensing this, Adam starts to turn into him for the escape. Jean Jacques then turns his body to his right as he circles the collar around Adam's neck and pulls on Adam's right shoulder, slightly turning Adam toward him.

3 Jean Jacques turns on all fours and fully allows Adam to turn into him while he completes circling his right elbow around Adam's neck. He is still controlling Adam's right elbow with his left hand.

4 Jean Jacques drives his right elbow toward the ground as he pushes his torso down on Adam's chest, flattening him to the mat and at the same time trapping his right arm. The choke will be accomplished by Jean Jacques continuing to drive his right elbow and shoulder toward the ground while driving Adam's right shoulder across his body.

Across-side to parallel collar choke

This technique can be employed from both the across-side position and the knee-on-stomach position. There are many options for the collars used in this attack. In this particular case, Jean Jacques chooses an initial position that works well from across-side. By wrapping your opponent's lapel around his own armpit and securing it with your arm that is wrapped around his head, you will greatly diminish your opponent's chance for an escape from the bottom. Note that since this hold will prevent your opponent from turning into you (since your shoulder will push against his chin and your right hand controls the lapel around his armpit), once in this position your opponent will generally have his arm up, waiting for a chance to escape.

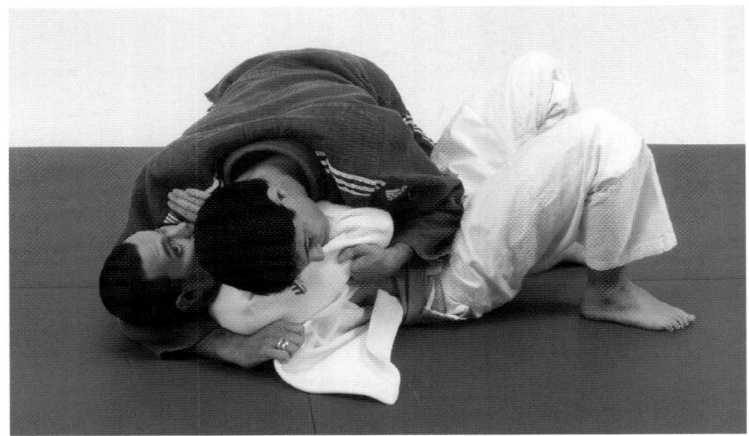

1 Jean Jacques is across-side. He uses his left arm to feed Adam's collar around the armpit and delivers it to his right hand, which is wrapped around Adam's head.

2 Since the hold is so solid, Jean Jacques opens space by moving his chest away from Adam, using his left hand to grip Adam's right collar. Many times your opponent will attempt to block that with one of his hands. If that happens, just pull back the attacking hand and try again until you succeed. Generally, as you back away, your opponent will momentarily relax, believing he has avoided the attack, and that lapse is the right moment to come back to the collar. If this doesn't work, you'll need to switch your attack to that demonstrated in position 25.

3 With the grip secure on both hands, Jean Jacques steps to his right and lifts his right arm, pushing Adam's head forward as he closes his elbows, choking Adam.

Detail

In this close-up one can see the proper way to apply the choke. Notice how Jean Jacques closes his elbows together, causing his forearms to choke Adam. It is also extremely important to straighten your right arm as much as possible. This will push your opponent's head forward and take away any space around the neck. If you were to keep your right elbow bent, it would create more space and the choke wouldn't cinch as tightly.

Across-side to parallel collar choke to arm lock

Position 24 alluded to the fact that when you go for a parallel collar choke, sometimes your opponent will use one or both or his hands to block the choke. It recommended removing your left hand and repeating the attack as your opponent relaxes, but that won't always work. Sometimes a wise or very defensive opponent won't let go of your attacking arm. This is the perfect moment to switch to an arm attack. The secret to advanced jiu-jitsu is the ability to smoothly transition from one move to the next as the options present themselves.

1 Jean Jacques attacks with the parallel choke, but Adam uses his left hand to block Jean Jacques's left elbow.

2 Jean Jacques steps forward with his right foot, still attempting to apply the choke, and pulls Adam over his left thigh.

3 Jean Jacques passes his right leg over his right arm and locks his right heel in Adam's armpit. Still holding Adam's collar with his right hand to make sure Adam can't turn toward him, Jean Jacques uses his left hand to pull Adam's left arm.

4 As he has complete control, with his heel locked in Adam's armpit, Jean Jacques can let go of his right-hand grip on Adam's collar, switch to having both hands on Adam's wrist, and fall back to an arm lock. Notice that Jean Jacques keeps his left knee up and close to Adam's elbow for two reasons: (1) to take away space and add pressure to the lock; and (2) if Adam somehow twists his arm away from the pressure, Jean Jacques can pull the arm across his left thigh and break it.

Across-side to Kimura

In position 25, Jean Jacques demonstrated how to transition from a collar choke to an arm lock as your opponent uses his hand to block the choke. Sometimes, however, an experienced opponent will lock his hands together, defending the arm lock as well. In that case, Jean Jacques, the master of variations, opts to apply a Kimura lock instead.

1 Jean Jacques attacks with the parallel choke, but Adam uses his left hand to block Jean Jacques's left elbow.

2 Jean Jacques steps forward with his right foot, while still attempting to apply the choke, and pulls Adam over his left thigh.

3 Jean Jacques passes his right leg over his right arm and locks his right heel in Adam's armpit, as in position 25. This time, however, Adam locks his hands to avoid the arm lock. With his right hand, Jean Jacques grabs Adam's left wrist. He wraps his left arm around Adam's left arm and holds his own right wrist with his left hand.

4 Jean Jacques turns his torso to the left, using the power of his entire upper body against Adam's hands, causing them to break open. He twists Adam's arm toward the left (or his back), applying pressure to the shoulder joint for the Kimura submission.

Across-side to taking the back

Here is yet another possibility deriving from the parallel collar choke in the across-side position. In this situation, your opponent blocks your choke with both hands, holding you near the elbow, making it very difficult for you to go for the arm lock (position 25) or the Kimura (position 26). But, for the versatile jiu-jitsu practitioner, there is always another option. Since the opponent has both hands engaged in blocking the choke, Jean Jacques chooses to take his back.

1 Jean Jacques attacks Adam's neck with the parallel collar choke. This time Adam defends by using both hands to block Jean Jacques's choking arm.

2 Jean Jacques lifts his left leg up and opens up his chest, while keeping his right knee close to Adam's body.

3 Jean Jacques sits back, pushing off his left leg, and pulls Adam up by his collar. Notice that Jean Jacques's right knee remains on the ground close to Adam's body. This facilitates placing the right hook to take the back.

4 Jean Jacques changes his left-hand grip from Adam's collar to his left sleeve as he continues to lean back while pulling Adam between his legs. Note that Jean Jacques's left heel, which was up, is the first to hook onto Adam's leg.

5 Jean Jacques places his right heel on Adam's right thigh for the second hook. It is very important to keep control of your opponent's gi until you get both hooks in. This will prevent him from shifting his weight to one of the sides. Since the correct way to escape a back hold is to shift your weight over to one side and place the back of your head to the ground, Jean Jacques uses his grip on Adam's gi to keep him centered between Jean Jacques's legs until Jean Jacques is ready to attack.

Parallel collar choke to arm lock 2

Although we mentioned in position 27 that it is difficult to achieve an arm lock when the opponent is using both hands to block the parallel collar choke, it is possible—especially if your opponent thinks you are going to take his back. This option is interchangeable with position 27. There is no inherent advantage to one over the other, but knowing them both means that you will be less predictable, especially with an opponent you have fought before.

1 Jean Jacques begins to take Adam's back (as in position 27), then switches and goes for an arm lock instead.

2 Jean Jacques throws his left leg over Adam's body for the cross-mount, keeping his right knee close to Adam's head. Jean Jacques also keeps his grip on Adam's gi for extra control.

3 Jean Jacques leans forward, lifting his hips slightly while using them to push Adam's left elbow forward.

4 Jean Jacques plants his right hand on the ground in front of Adam's face. This has two purposes: (1) Jean Jacques will place his weight on it and pivot off it; and (2) the hand will block Adam from spinning counter-clockwise to prevent Jean Jacques from swinging his right leg over Adam's head. Note how Jean Jacques uses his hips and left arm to trap Adam's left arm.

5 Jean Jacques passes his right leg in front of Adam's head and falls back for the arm lock.

Across-side to mount 1: triangle finish

The mount is an extremely important position in jiu-jitsu. Since it is a dominant position, many attacks originate from it. Because of that, your opponent will prevent you from attaining it at all costs. In the following techniques, Jean Jacques demonstrates a clever way to attain the mount from the across-side position, along with a variety of submission possibilities to go for once you are there.

1 Jean Jacques is across-side and starts to slide his left knee onto Kid's stomach to mount him. Kid blocks the knee with his right hand to prevent Jean Jacques from attaining the mount.

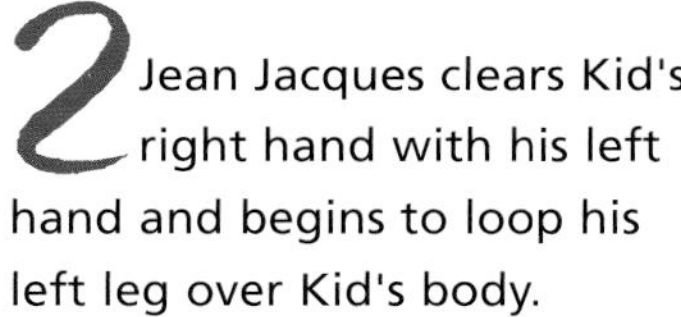

2 Jean Jacques clears Kid's right hand with his left hand and begins to loop his left leg over Kid's body.

3 Jean Jacques achieves the mount as his left foot touches the ground. As soon as he does that, he reaches back and grabs Kid's right hand with his left one.

4 Jean Jacques slides his left knee up toward Kid's head, pulls Kid's right arm up with his left hand, and pulls Kid's left elbow with his right hand.

5 Pushing off his right foot, Jean Jacques starts to fall to his left and pulls Kid with him, tricking Kid into thinking he is escaping from the bottom (such as in an upa, or bridge, motion).

6 Kid falls right into Jean Jacques's triangle, as Jean Jacques figure-fours his leg around Kid's neck and left arm. To complete the submission and apply greater pressure to the choke, Jean Jacques will push Kid's left arm across his body to his left.

7 Jean Jacques uses both hands to pull Kid's head toward him as he squeezes the neck by bringing his knees together for the triangle choke.

Across-side to mount 2: arm lock

In the previous technique, Jean Jacques demonstrated how to achieve a triangle choke submission from the mount. Here, he opts for an arm lock, instead. Generally, if an opponent raises his head while mounted and has proper posture, it becomes more difficult to get the triangle, and you should go for the arm lock. If his head is close to his body, then the triangle is the better option.

1 Jean Jacques reaches the mount, as in position 29. He lifts his right leg and pulls on Kid's shoulder while bracing with his left arm.

2 Jean Jacques raises his torso and pulls on Kid's left arm with both hands. Notice that Jean Jacques locks his right elbow around Kid's left arm, trapping Kid's elbow as well as locking Kid's left hand in his armpit.

3 Jean Jacques places both his hands on Kid's left elbow and pulls the elbow toward his torso as he raises his body for the submission.

Across-side to mount 3: Omoplata

The straight arm lock in position 30 only works if your opponent's elbow is pointing toward yours and his arm is straight, so you can apply pressure on the elbow by pulling it toward your side. If the defender reacts by twisting his wrist down, his arm bends and his elbow points up instead of away, and the arm lock won't work. In that case, you need to switch to an Omoplata, or shoulder lock.

1 Jean Jacques reaches the mount, as in position 29. He lifts his right leg and pulls on Kid's shoulder while bracing with his left arm. Because Kid twists his wrist clockwise to avoid an arm lock, Jean Jacques chooses to go for the Omoplata.

2 Jean Jacques leans back with his torso and starts to pass his right leg over Kid's head.

3 Still bracing with his left arm, Jean Jacques controls Kid's left elbow with his right hand as he has his right leg in front of Kid's head, grapevining Kid's left arm.

4 Jean Jacques figure-fours his leg around Kid's arm, left leg over his right foot, locking the position. At the same time, he reaches with his right hand and holds Kid's belt to prevent him from rolling forward for the escape. Jean Jacques will submit Kid by thrusting his hips forward, applying pressure to Kid's left shoulder.

Across-side to arm lock 5: same-side arm

The traditional arm-lock attack from across-side involves an attack on the arm opposite the side you are dominating. You use your arm to loop your opponent's opposite arm, controlling it, and then circle over your opponent's head and pass your leg over for the submission. The problem with that attack is that as you spin around to take the arm it allows the defender more opportunity to counter by yanking his elbow down and out of the lock. Jean Jacques avoids that here by going for the quicker and more direct submission. Ironically, this attack is even easier to defend—the opponent can turn to his left and pull his elbow out as well. For this attack to work, it is imperative that you control your opponent's left arm and also that you surprise him: he is expecting the attack on the opposite side and won't be guarding against this move.

1 Jean Jacques is across-side on Kid with his hips switched in a controlling position. His left hand is under Kid's right arm and his right hand holds Kid's left arm.

2 Pushing off his right foot, Jean Jacques scoots his hips back, creating space between his left knee and Kid's left armpit. This is a key moment in the technique, as the space is what enables Jean Jacques's direct-attack version of the arm lock.

3 Jean Jacques slides his left knee into the space he created, as he pulls Kid's left arm up and leans back with his torso. At this point Jean Jacques is pushing his hips up off the ground, setting up his next move. Notice that Kid's left arm is already between Jean Jacques's legs and in perfect position for the arm lock.

4 Having his hips off the ground allows Jean Jacques to quickly pass his right leg over Kid's face and fall back for the arm lock.

Across-side to Omoplata 2

The Omoplata, or shoulder lock, is rarely used from the across-side position, being easier to employ when you have your opponent in your guard or on all fours. But that is precisely why Jean Jacques uses this attack in competition with a high rate of success—no one expects it. It is difficult to pull off, however, and will take time and practice to perfect. Once you achieve it, though, the results will be worth it. Jean Jacques also demonstrates an arm-lock submission from the same position.

1 Jean Jacques is across-side with his hips twisted, his back facing Kid's face. This is a common setup to transfer to the mounted position. Jean Jacques holds Kid's right knee with his right hand, as if he is preparing to loop his right leg over Kid's body for the mount. At this point, Kid is holding Jean Jacques's right hip with his right hand to prevent this action. Note that Jean Jacques's left knee is close to Kid's hips to take away space and prevent Kid from replacing the guard with his right leg by escaping the hip.

2 Pushing off his right foot, Jean Jacques raises his hips off the ground and slides his left knee back toward Kid's head. Kid holds on to Jean Jacques's right leg in anticipation of the mount.

3 Jean Jacques changes his right-hand grip from Kid's knee to his right hand and pulls it between his legs.

4 Using the element of surprise, Jean Jacques raises his torso and slides his left calf under Kid's right arm near the armpit, while still keeping some of his weight on his left hand next to Kid's hips to keep Kid from scooting away.

5 Jean Jacques rolls forward over his shoulder while still holding Kid's right arm. Note that if your opponent successfully blocks this maneuver, you'll need to switch to the attack in position 34.

6 Jean Jacques ends up in the classic Omoplata position, legs in a figure-four (right leg over the left foot) around Kid's right arm. He will continue to roll his hips forward to apply pressure on Kid's shoulder for the Omoplata submission.

6 (option) An optional attack from the same position: rather than rolling his hips forward, Jean Jacques passes his right shin under Kid's chin and pushes Kid's right arm up against Jean Jacques's left calf, applying pressure to the elbow for an arm lock.

Across-side to triangle

When attempting to go straight from the across-side position to an Omoplata finish, you run the risk of your opponent keeping his chest and head up in good posture as you attempt to roll, preventing you from achieving the Omoplata. A skilled opponent may also use his right hand to grab his own belt, making it very difficult to break the grip and complete the submission. Being one of the most technical fighters in the world, Jean Jacques prefers the certainty of a triangle choke rather than trying to overpower the grip.

1 Jean Jacques's roll to the shoulder lock is properly defended by Kid, who has his head up and torso straight, blocking the continuation of the movement. The opponent will often also be holding his belt with his right hand.

2 Jean Jacques opens his legs and moves his hips to his left. Notice Kid's right arm is still trapped.

34

3 Jean Jacques places his right calf over Kid's left shoulder and presses down on it. This is very important to keep Kid from being able to again foil the move by straightening his torso. Jean Jacques also presses his left leg on Kid's back to keep him tight. Jean Jacques uses both his hands and pulls Kid's right elbow forward, causing him to either let go of the grip around his belt or submit due to the pressure on his shoulder.

4 As Kid lets go of the grip, Jean Jacques pulls Kid's arm across his body with both his hands and scoots his hips to the left. Again, notice the pressure applied by Jean Jacques's right calf on Kid's shoulder, keeping him from straightening his body.

5 Jean Jacques closes his legs in a figure-four (left leg over the right foot) for the triangle choke and applies the choking pressure by pulling Kid's head toward him with both hands as he closes his knees.

Across-side to toe hold

This is a variation on position 33, ending in a toe hold instead of a shoulder lock. The attacks are equally effective and completely interchangeable, so the choice of which to use has more to do with personal preference than strategy. Different attacks fit different styles. Remember, however, that to be a submission expert you have to master enough options to always have a place to go, but as you are learning, make sure you really get each position before moving on to the next. It is more important to master some techniques very well and be able to execute them perfectly than to know hundreds of submissions and not know when or how to apply them.

1 Using the same moves as in position 34, Jean Jacques again has his left leg under Kid's right arm, while pulling Kid's right hand with his own right hand between his legs. At this point, rather than rolling forward and going for the shoulder lock, as he did in position 33, Jean Jacques opts to go for the toe hold.

2 Balancing his left hand on the ground, Jean Jacques pushes off his right foot and falls to the mat, pulling Kid by the arm along with him.

3 Jean Jacques lands on the opposite side of Kid with his right arm still between his legs and both legs over Kid's head. At this point Jean Jacques's right leg blocks Kid's head, impeding him from rolling toward his left and ending up on top.

4 Jean Jacques crosses his legs in a figure-four (right leg over left foot) around Kid's right arm and spins his body to the left, attacking Kid's right foot with a toe hold by holding Kid's toes with his left hand and completing the lock by circling his right hand around Kid's foot and grabbing his left wrist. The pressure is applied with the left hand pulling the toes for the submission.

4 (option) As an option, Jean Jacques may push on Kid's right hand with his own left hand, while using his right hand to pull on Kid's elbow for another shoulder lock.

Across-side to lapel choke

Jean Jacques's game doesn't rely on the gi, but he certainly knows how to take advantage of the cloth when the opportunity presents itself. Here, he demonstrates a choke from the across-side position in which he uses his own lapel to choke the opponent. The key here is to be subtle when passing the lapel over your opponent's head; if you use too much pressure you will attract his attention to the move and he'll be more apt to defend it.

1 Jean Jacques is across-side with his hips facing Kid. He opens his right lapel, as close to the end as possible.

2 Jean Jacques passes his lapel in front of Kid's head, feeding it to his left hand.

3 Jean Jacques passes his right arm around the back of Kid's head and receives the lapel back from his left hand.

4 Using his left hand to control Kid's right shoulder, Jean Jacques pushes off his right foot and raises his torso slightly to create space as he begins to straighten his right arm.

5 Jean Jacques squares his hips and slips his right knee between his right arm and Kid's body. He will apply a tremendous pressure for the choke by straightening his torso and driving his knee forward while pulling on his own lapel with his right hand.

Across-side head-and-arm choke

Often when you are across-side, your opponent will use his arms to try to push you away. The general rule is to switch your hips and deflect his force. There are, however, a few instances where a submission is possible. Watch for your opponent to expose his arm or forget to defend his collar. If your hips are facing the opponent's head and he is pushing back with both arms, you have a shot at applying a head-and-arm choke.

1 Jean Jacques is across-side on Kid with his hips facing Kid's head. Kid is trying to escape by using both hands to push Jean Jacques away. If unopposed, he will escape the hips to his right as he pushes Jean Jacques's torso back, until he reverses the position. To foil this, Jean Jacques knives his right hand between his chest and Kid's left arm.

2 Jean Jacques drives his forearm into Kid's left biceps near the elbow (for better leverage), deflecting the push on his chest. Note that Jean Jacques uses not simply his arm strength but his entire chest to help push Kid's arm down and away from him. This is very important as you may face an opponent who is stronger than you and you cannot win a battle of arm strength alone.

3 Jean Jacques loops his right leg over Kid's left arm and traps it. Notice Jean Jacques grips his left knee with his right hand to keep Kid's arm from escaping, until he can trap it solidly with his right leg. From here, if Kid does not block the arm, Jean Jacques can apply a submission by switching legs and trapping Kid's arm with his left (or lower) leg, causing pressure to the shoulder or elbow.

4 Faced with this situation, a smart opponent will reach over and grab his left hand with his right to defend the arm.

5 Jean Jacques reaches behind Kid's head with his right arm, using his chest to trap Kid's right arm and shoulder across his own body.

6 Jean Jacques locks both hands together and applies the choke by pulling his arms together while driving his chest into Kid, much like a triangle choke or the traditional kata-gatame choke.

Across-side to collar choke: defender rolls away

Rolling away from the attacker is a common way to escape from the across-side position. If the defender can get some separation between his chest and the attacker's chest, he can roll his body away from under the attacker, generally going to his knees. This position demonstrates a quick method for dealing with such a situation. The attack can also be used even without the opponent attempting to escape. You would use your chest to push your opponent's left shoulder up until he turns sideways; then you would proceed as in step 1.

1 As Kid starts to roll away, Jean Jacques quickly grabs Kid's collar with his left hand and circles Kid's neck with his right.

2 Jean Jacques feeds Kid's collar to his right hand, making sure he grips as close to the neck as possible. The tighter the grip here, the faster the choke will take effect. Jean Jacques uses a special trick to make sure he gets as tight a grip on the collar as possible: With his left hand, Jean Jacques straightens Kid's collar by pulling it down and slides his right hand up on it.

3 Jean Jacques circles his left hand around Kid's left arm until the back of his hand touches the back of Kid's head. Jean Jacques will apply the choking pressure by pulling up on his right hand as he straightens his left forearm, sliding it on the back of Kid's head.

One good way to picture the choking motion here is to envision that Jean Jacques's left hand is gripping a bow, while his right hand is holding the arrow. He executes the same motion as he would to tense the bow.

Across-side double attack

This is the same attack as in position 38, but here the opponent blocks the choke with his hand. Even though the double attack is a relatively common attack, it is the finesse of the executioner that renders this a devastating technique. You need to go for the choke with the intent to submit, while at the same time preparing for the arm lock by properly positioning your body.

1 Jean Jacques attempts to feed Kid's collar to his right hand, but Kid uses his right hand to hold Jean Jacques's right wrist, taking away the choke.

2 Sensing that the choke is being blocked by Kid, Jean Jacques continues as if he is proceeding with the choke, but instead adjusts his left knee on Kid's rib and uses his left arm to trap Kid's arm.

3 Jean Jacques pushes Kid's face down with his right hand as he raises his body.

4 Jean Jacques passes his right leg in front of Kid's face. Notice Jean Jacques is putting all his weight on his right hand, which is pushing down on Kid's face, making it easy for him to pivot his body over Kid. The hand on Kid's face controls the chin and keeps Kid from rolling to his left and yanking his left elbow away from Jean Jacques's control.

5 Jean Jacques falls back for the arm lock.

Across-side double attack 2: opponent blocks choke

When going for the double attack, if your opponent not only uses his right hand on your right wrist to prevent the choking pressure, but also grabs his left collar with his left hand, making it more difficult to go for the arm lock, you can add a little twist and submit him with this devastating and powerful choke.

1 Jean Jacques is attempting the collar choke, but Kid defends it by holding Jean Jacques's right wrist with his right hand and holding his own left collar with his left hand. Since the left hand is already secured, it would be much more difficult for Jean Jacques to take the left arm in an arm lock.

2 Instead of fighting for the arm, Jean Jacques slides his right knee between his own right arm and Kid's left shoulder.

3 Jean Jacques pulls up on Kid's collar with his right arm as he pushes Kid's head down with his right shin, applying a tremendous amount of pressure to the choke. Notice that Jean Jacques uses his left hand holding the right lapel in front of Kid's body to keep him from rolling to his right and negating some of the choking pressure.

Across-side double attack 3: Kimura option

To have an advanced game, you need to have as many options in your arsenal as possible, because your opponent will have learned how to deal with all the standard ones. Here is another double-attack option you can use when your opponent blocks the choke with both hands. In the case of the double attack, the advanced opponent is prepared for the choke-armlock combination, so the Kimura alternative adds another element of danger to the scene.

1 Jean Jacques is attempting a collar choke, but Kid defends it by holding Jean Jacques's right wrist with his right hand and holding his own left collar with his left hand. Securing the left hand makes it much more difficult for Jean Jacques to take Kid's left arm in an arm lock.

2 Jean Jacques steps forward with his right leg, placing his right foot just over Kid's head. He removes his right hand from around Kid's head and grabs Kid's left wrist. He uses his own left hand to grab his right wrist, securing the Kimura grip.

3 Jean Jacques kneels down with his right knee as he raises his left knee up. Notice that he is now 180 degrees from his opponent and his legs are preventing Kid's torso from moving.

4 Jean Jacques yanks Kid's left hand from the collar and leads it to his left.

5 Jean Jacques moves Kid's left arm to his back for the shoulder lock. Notice that in both this and the previous step, Jean Jacques uses the power of his upper body to drive Kid's arm in the proper direction, making it virtually impossible for even the strongest of opponents to resist with arm strength alone.

Choke from the back

Having the opponent's back is perhaps the most valuable position in Brazilian jiu-jitsu. From there you can use a variety of chokes and other submissions. The most important thing to keep in mind when you get your opponent's back is of course not to lose the position. The second thing is that, in order to keep the position, you should attack your opponent's neck. If the opponent is not under the stress of an attack, he is much more apt to escape.

1 Jean Jacques has Kid's back, both hooks in place, and is ready to attack. His right arm is over Kid's shoulder while his left is under Kid's armpit to assist in the leverage for the choke. His right hand is delivering Kid's collar to his left one.

2 Here, Jean Jacques has achieved the proper hand position for the choke: right hand on the collar, as high as possible, and left hand on the opposite collar.

3 Jean Jacques will apply the choking pressure by pulling his right hand back while straightening his left arm, pulling the opposite collar down, in a bow-and-arrow motion.

4 Here is a variation that sometimes occurs: Kid reacts more quickly than before and uses his right hand to grab Jean Jacques's right wrist, somewhat blocking the choke. Note the proper posture of Kid's right arm as he keeps his elbow close to his chest for extra leverage.

5 Sensing that he needs an extra "boost" of power for the choke to work, Jean Jacques opens his right leg, releasing the hook, and spins his body to his left while he straightens his left arm behind Kid's neck.

6 Jean Jacques reaches maximum power by leaning back as his body reaches a right angle with Kid's body, adding a great deal of pressure to the choke.

Double attack from the back

The double attack from the back is a variation of the previous attack. Jean Jacques switched to the double attack because his opponent defended the choke with his right hand, grabbing Jean Jacques's wrist early enough that Jean Jacques could no longer add enough "octane" to the choke by spinning his body. Jean Jacques adds a little variation to the position by trapping his opponent's arm with his leg. From there, he can return to the choke or change to an arm lock.

1 Jean Jacques attempts the collar choke, but Kid blocks it, his right hand holding Jean Jacques's right wrist early enough that Jean Jacques can't get a good enough grip on Kid's collar to try one of the two previous choke options.

2 Jean Jacques releases his right-hand grip on Kid's collar. The natural reaction to the sudden release of the collar is for Kid to continue gripping the attacking arm as he wants to control it and keep it off his collar. Jean Jacques uses that to open Kid's arm.

3 Jean Jacques loops Kid's arm with his right leg.

4 Having cleared the way with his leg, Jean Jacques returns to the choke, his right hand on Kid's collar.

5 Alternatively, Jean Jacques may opt for an arm lock. Instead of using his right hand to grab Kid's collar, he can use it to grab Kid's right arm along with the left hand that was already looped around the arm as he falls back.

6 Jean Jacques then places his left leg over Kid's midsection and applies pressure by lifting his hips.

Omoplata from the turtle position

The "turtle," or all-fours, position is a very common defensive position in Brazilian jiu-jitsu. A defender will use it following an escape from the bottom, or to avoid a guard pass. The attacker has a few options, as Jean Jacques demonstrates in this series of techniques. Here, he goes for an Omoplata, or shoulder lock. The most common attack from this position is the clock choke (see position 46); cagey opponents will defend that first and sometimes ignore the arm closest to the attacker. That is the time to go for the Omoplata. Generally speaking, the sooner you start to attack the opponent as he turns turtle, the better, because if given time he will try to close all the gaps for hooks and grips.

1 Kid has turned turtle and Jean Jacques is on his side. To control Kid and keep him from rolling over and replacing the guard or slipping toward the back, Jean Jacques puts his weight on Kid's back, pushing his chest down on it. At the same time, he grabs Kid's left wrist with his right hand and grapevines his left arm around Kid's left arm.

2 With his right hand Jean Jacques grabs Kid's right arm and drives it between his legs until he hooks it with his left calf.

3 Having securely trapped Kid's arm with his calf, Jean Jacques will roll forward over his left shoulder.

4 As Jean Jacques rolls forward, Kid must accompany the roll to relieve pressure on his shoulder. Note: Be careful when practicing this position with a partner. Roll slowly and make sure your partner is aware and capable of following the roll with you, or else he may injure his shoulder.

5 As he completes the forward roll, Jean Jacques crosses his legs in a figure-four around Kid's arm and sits up.

6 Jean Jacques grabs Kid's right pant leg with his right hand. At this point he may release the figure-four lock on his legs in order to sit up.

7 Jean Jacques will submit Kid by continuing to move his hips forward, applying pressure to Kid's shoulder joint.

Taking the back of the turtle

Although it seems like it would be the easiest thing in the world to take your opponent's back when he is in the turtle position, it can actually be rather difficult. Any attempt to place hooks will be met with the opponent either closing the gap between his thigh and body, or simply blocking the hook with his arm. This technique demonstrates a few secrets that will help you succeed in taking the back.

1 Again, Jean Jacques starts on the side of Kid, who has turned turtle. Jean Jacques has his right knee up and right foot firmly planted on the mat away from Kid's body, while his left knee is planted just behind Kid's right knee. With the weight of his chest pressing on top of Kid's back, Jean Jacques places his left arm around Kid's waist so that the palm of his hand is touching the inside of Kid's left thigh. Getting this penetration is essential to making this attack work. If you can't get inside, you'll need to switch to position 47.

2 Jean Jacques switches stance, throwing his left leg over to Kid's opposite side and placing his right knee where his left one was (just behind Kid's right knee). Jean Jacques braces Kid's right arm with his own right hand and begins to roll over his right shoulder, bringing Kid with him. Notice that Kid's right side is completely blocked by Jean Jacques's right hand and knee, making it impossible for Kid to avoid rolling with him.

3 As he continues the roll, Jean Jacques opens Kid's left leg with his arm and throws his left leg over Kid's leg to place one hook.

4 Jean Jacques releases the right hand that was on Kid's arm and grabs Kid's left collar.

5 Jean Jacques then uses the left hand that was on Kid's thigh to grab Kid's right collar. He will choke by pulling his right hand up and his left one down, pulling the collar tight.

Clock choke

The ingenious clock choke, if correctly applied, will quickly submit an opponent in the turtle position, due to the tremendous choking pressure on the neck. The clock choke works extremely well when applied as follows: you are passing the guard and your opponent turns to all fours to avoid the completion of the pass. You should attack the collar just as the opponent begins to turn, so by the time he gets to all fours you already have control of his collar, ready for the choke. It is more difficult to apply the choke if you don't yet have the collar when your opponent gets on all fours and protects his neck. Many times as you attempt to take the back, your opponent will forget about his collar, giving you the chance to go for the clock choke. To make it effective, however, you need to concentrate on controlling the opposite side of your opponent so he can't turn into you once you have one hand on the collar. Additionally, the deeper your hand grabs on the collar, the quicker and more effective the choke will be. So it is important to adjust your grip at the same time as you secure control of your opponent's side. You can adjust and tighten the choke simply by crawling your fingers up the collar as you and your opponent struggle for control, as Jean Jacques demonstrates here.

1 Jean Jacques is on the side of Kid, who has turned turtle. This time he has his hands grabbing Kid's collar, around each side of his body.

2 Jean Jacques releases his right-hand grip on the collar and places his right arm around Kid's neck.

3 With his left hand, Jean Jacques passes Kid's left collar to his right hand. Once he has a firm grip on the left collar, he will use his left hand to grab Kid's right collar. One variation of the clock choke has the attacker grab the defender's left arm with his left hand, but Jean Jacques prefers to hold both sides of the collar so he can apply more pressure to the neck. Note that Jean Jacques maintains pressure with his chest on Kid's back at all times so Kid can't roll forward and replace the guard.

4 Jean Jacques shoots his left foot out as he moves his hips forward, bringing his bodyweight forward on Kid. He will add pressure to the choke by pushing off his right foot as he drives his hips forward. The further forward he moves his hips, the more pressure the choke will have. The torque created by the body going forward is what causes the devastating pressure of the clock choke. Many practitioners incorrectly apply the clock choke by either leaning back with their body 90 degrees to the opponent's or by simply pulling the collar up with the arm, both of which greatly diminish the effectiveness of the submission.

Taking the back of the turtle 2: falling to the side

Position 45 demonstrated how to attack the turtle position by taking your opponent's back. Key to success there is reacting quickly, before your opponent has had the chance to close himself so tightly that you can't slip your arm to the inside of his thigh. If you are late in taking the back of the turtle, you will need to use a slightly different approach, falling to the opposite side.

1 Jean Jacques is on the side of Kid, who has turned turtle. This time, however, Kid has closed himself very tightly, making it more difficult to apply one of the previous techniques. Jean Jacques grabs the back of Kid's gi with his right hand and Kid's belt with his left.

2 Jean Jacques springs to his feet by putting his weight on his left arm, which is holding the belt, and pulling up with his right hand. Notice that it is very important to keep the pressure on Kid's belt (hips); this will actually lock him in position and prevent him from attempting any escape.

3 Jean Jacques steps over Kid's body with his left leg and begins to pull Kid by the collar over to the side, while still pinning Kid's hips down with his left hand.

4 Jean Jacques continues the motion and pulls Kid's collar with his right hand as he pushes Kid's hips with his left arm, causing Kid to fall to his lap. Since Jean Jacques's left foot was planted on the ground next to Kid's left hip, his left hook is automatically in place.

5 Jean Jacques hooks his right leg over Kid's right arm, slipping his right hand around Kid's neck to pull the collar tight and grapevining his left arm around Kid's left arm, with his hand touching the back of Kid's head. Jean Jacques is ready to apply the choke.

Guard wing sweep

The strength of this sweep is the fact that it presents quite a few variations. The most commonly used is the scissors sweep, in which the attacker scissors his legs, causing the opponent to be reversed toward his right. In this case, however, the opponent braced himself to his right with his right hand, preventing being knocked to his right, so Jean Jacques opts for the wing sweep.

1 Jean Jacques has Bryce in his closed guard, with his right hand deep in Bryce's collar and his left hand controlling Bryce's left arm.

2 Jean Jacques opens his guard and switches his hips, placing his left leg on the ground just in front of Bryce's right leg, blocking it. His right shin is in front of Bryce's stomach and his right foot is hooking the side of Bryce's body. He tries a scissors sweep, but Bryce blocks it by bracing with his right arm.

3 Jean Jacques switches his right hand from Bryce's collar to his belt as he sits up, bracing his right shin against Bryce's hips.

4 Jean Jacques falls back to the mat and uses that momentum to pull Bryce by the belt. He pulls Bryce across his body by the left sleeve and opens his right leg.

5 With Bryce's entire weight on his right shin, Jean Jacques easily sweeps him by opening his right leg as he continues to pull Bryce's left arm across.

6 Jean Jacques finishes the move across the side for the sweep.

Taking the back from the scissors sweep

This is one of Jean Jacques's favorite techniques, as he relishes being on an opponent's back for a submission. As in the previous position, Jean Jacques has tried the scissors sweep and the opponent defended it by bracing himself with his right arm. Jean Jacques then switched to the wing sweep, but the opponent countered again by lowering his chest on Jean Jacques's leg, taking away the leverage for the sweep.

1 Jean Jacques tries to apply the wing sweep, but Bryce counters by lowering his weight onto Jean Jacques's right leg.

2 At this point, Jean Jacques places his left foot on Bryce's right knee and slides his own hips toward Bryce's body, simultaneously pulling Bryce's left arm across his body with his left hand.

3 Jean Jacques pushes Bryce's right knee open with his left foot, pulls Bryce's left arm open, and slides his right leg out and around Bryce's body. He pulls Bryce forward with his right hand. At this point you can clearly see that Bryce is completely exposed and Jean Jacques can easily take his back.

4 Jean Jacques does that by looping his right leg around Bryce's body and locking in the right hook on Bryce's hips.

5 To further dominate the position, Jean Jacques flattens Bryce down on the mat by pressing down with his hips on Bryce's back.

Arm lock from the scissors sweep

Like a game of chess, Brazilian jiu-jitsu is a dynamic art that involves two thinking humans reacting to each other's moves. You can't follow the same rigid steps to the same submission every time. Instead, you must master many options that can flow together and then link them as the situation requires, based on your opponent's reactions. Here, Jean Jacques tried the scissors sweep, but his opponent braced himself and then lowered his hips on Jean Jacques's thigh, preventing the wing sweep, so Jean Jacques can either go to the back as he showed in position 49 or he can go directly to a submission. His opponent's reaction to the sweep will decide for him. Sometimes as you pull on your opponent's left arm, he senses the danger of the arm lock and reacts by closing his elbow. Even when you manage to control and expose his left arm, he may close his right arm tight and preclude you from locking your right foot over for the lock. You must pay attention to these two keys and react quickly when the opportunity arises to apply the submission. If your opponent closes his right arm tight but leaves his head on the mat, you can throw your right leg over it and hook it under the chin for the arm lock as well.

1 Jean Jacques tries to apply the wing sweep, but Bryce counters by lowering his weight on Jean Jacques's right leg.

2 At this point, Jean Jacques places his left foot on Bryce's right knee and slides his own hips toward Bryce's body, simultaneously pulling Bryce's left arm across his body with his own left hand.

3 Jean Jacques pushes Bryce's right knee open with his left foot, pulls Bryce's left arm open, and slides his right leg out and around Bryce's body. He also pulls Bryce forward with his right hand. At this point, Bryce is completely exposed and Jean Jacques could easily take the back. However, because Bryce allowed Jean Jacques to control his left arm and open it, it became vulnerable to an arm lock. Additionally, Bryce did not close his opposite arm tight to prevent Jean Jacques from hooking his right foot in, so everything is in place for Jean Jacques to go for a submission.

4 Jean Jacques throws his right leg over Bryce, but rather than hooking around Bryce's hip, he loops high toward Bryce's head.

5 Jean Jacques hooks his right foot under Bryce's right arm, which was bracing on the mat, following it by rotating his hips toward his left and using both hands to grab Bryce's left arm.

6 Jean Jacques continues rotating his body until his head touches the ground. He uses it to help lift his body up so he can push his hips down on Bryce's elbow for the arm lock. Many practitioners err in this position by turning their bodies completely until their face is on the mat. That will cause your entire body to be on the mat and will diminish your ability to apply pressure by bringing your hips down.

Butterfly guard sweep

The butterfly guard, or sitting guard with hooks, should be an important piece in the arsenal of every advanced Brazilian jiu-jitsu practitioner. To sweep an opponent from the butterfly guard, the most important things to remember are not to have your back on the ground and to slide your hips to one of the sides or hooks. In this case, Jean Jacques shows the basic sweep with a slight variation: he lassoes his opponent's right arm.

1 Jean Jacques is in the butterfly guard and has lassoed Bryce's right arm with his left one. He uses his right arm to pull down on Bryce's gi and deliver it to his left hand, giving him a much tighter grip around Bryce's arm. Jean Jacques slides his hips to his left, indicating a sweep to the right. Anticipating that, Bryce braces himself with his left arm.

2 Jean Jacques grabs Bryce's left arm with his right one as he starts the sweeping action by throwing his body to the right and lifting Bryce's right leg with his left hooks.

3 Jean Jacques continues to "fall" to his right until his forehead touches the ground. He pulls Bryce's left arm toward his head, removing the "brace."

4 Without an arm to stop the motion, Bryce is swept. It is very important to notice Jean Jacques's sweeping motion. He doesn't fall to the side, but rather aims his forehead to a point on the ground that is at a 45-degree angle to his body. Many practitioners err by attempting to sweep all the way to the side instead of to 45 degrees, in which case the sweep will generally fail and the two fighters will end up struggling sideways on the mat.

5 Jean Jacques ends the sweep mounted on Bryce.

Butterfly guard sweep to triangle choke

As in position 51, Jean Jacques attempts a butterfly guard sweep. This time, however, the opponent gives himself a wide brace with his left arm, making it very difficult for Jean Jacques to pull his arm and remove the brace. However, what distinguishes truly great jiu-jitsu practitioners is their ability to see opportunity within setbacks. Always looking for a submission, Jean Jacques takes advantage of the space Bryce has left open with his brace and goes for a triangle choke.

1 Much like in the previous position, Jean Jacques is in the butterfly guard, with Bryce's right arm lassoed by his left one, and grabs Bryce's left wrist with his right hand as he starts the sweeping motion.

2 As he begins to fall to his right for the sweep, the crafty Bryce follows the sweep with his hips and opens his left arm wide to brace himself solidly.

3 As you can see, at this point the sweep won't work as Bryce is firmly balanced.

4 With so much space between himself and Bryce, Jean Jacques is free to pull his right leg up until he can slide his right foot in front of Bryce's left arm. It is very important to keep your opponent up in the air by continuing to raise your left leg in an attempt to sweep him, otherwise he won't worry about defending the sweep and will be more apt to pull his arms in and avoid the triangle.

5 As he passes his leg around Bryce's arm and goes for the triangle choke, Jean Jacques shifts his hips to the right and releases the pressure on his left leg.

6 Jean Jacques crosses his legs in a figure-four, left leg over the right foot, trapping Bryce's right arm and head inside the triangle.

7 Jean Jacques submits Bryce by pulling Bryce's right arm across his body and pulling on Bryce's head with both hands as he squeezes his knees together, cinching the noose.

Butterfly guard sweep to arm lock

Here are another couple of great variations for submissions from the butterfly guard sweep when your opponent braces his arm far from you. The first option is to go for an inverted arm lock. Should your opponent spin his wrist to defend the arm lock, you can transfer to a shoulder lock (Omoplata). These work best when your opponent moves so far forward that it would be a stretch for you to bring your hip around for the triangle. Some people also find that they simply execute the Omoplata better than the triangle.

1 Jean Jacques attempts a butterfly guard sweep to his right, but Bryce blocks it by bracing his left hand on the mat far away.

2 Jean Jacques places his right foot on Bryce's hips and uses it to slide his hips out and away from Bryce. Notice that Jean Jacques maintains control of Bryce's right arm, his left arm grapevined around it while holding Bryce's collar.

3 Jean Jacques continues to slide his hips and turns his body to the right while putting his left knee on Bryce's back and pressing Bryce's right elbow down with his left thigh and knee for the inverted arm lock.

4 If Bryce spins his wrist to escape the inverted arm lock, Jean Jacques will then continue to turn to his right and throw his left leg over Bryce's body around his right arm. Note that Jean Jacques is holding Bryce's right arm with his left hand to keep him from removing it from the lock.

5 Jean Jacques grabs Bryce's hips with his left hand, to stop him from rolling forward for the escape, while at the same time he switches his legs and pushes forward with his hips for the shoulder lock.

Closed guard arm-lock variation

The normal arm lock from inside the closed guard generally involves sliding your hips to one side and passing your leg on that side over your opponent's shoulder and in front of his face while raising your hips. This advanced variation, however, demonstrates a quicker way to achieve the same result. It is easier to achieve the submission with this option because your leg does not have to go around your opponent's head, just over one of his shoulders. The disadvantage? It is easy for your opponent to defend this attack by wriggling his shoulder back in between your legs. You have to be quick and have the finesse to "climb" your legs over and lock the shoulder.

1 Jean Jacques has Bryce in his closed guard. Bryce has both hands on Jean Jacques's collar and is in good position, with his back straight and his head up. Jean Jacques holds both sleeves around the elbows to prepare for his move.

2 Since he wants to arm lock Bryce's right arm, he opens his legs and slides his hips to his left as he pushes Bryce's right elbow in with his left hand and pulls Bryce's left elbow out with his right hand, breaking Bryce's hold and bringing him down closer to him. Jean Jacques also raises his hips to set up the next step.

3 Jean Jacques throws his left leg over Bryce's right shoulder and locks it in place with his right foot. He also pulls forward on Bryce's left elbow to help bring him even closer. Notice how Jean Jacques's hips are now set tightly under Bryce's right arm.

4 Jean Jacques grabs Bryce's right wrist with both hands and lifts his hips for the arm lock, applying pressure to the elbow joint.

Closed guard arm-lock variation: Omoplata

In a continuation from the previous position, once Jean Jacques achieves the lock over the opponent's shoulder (see position 54, step 3) he can either go for the arm lock shown in position 54 or he can apply a few different variations. Here are two such options: the key lock and the Omoplata. The key lock is useful when your opponent defends his arm by pushing his weight forward and bending you back. The Omoplata is handy if your opponent defends the arm locks but leaves his left elbow open.

1 Jean Jacques has achieved the lock over Bryce's right shoulder with his left leg crossed over it and locked under his right foot. He could attack Bryce's arm for an arm lock, but in this case Bryce is able to defend by pulling himself forward with his left hand on Jean Jacques's gi collar.

2 Jean Jacques switches to a key lock by driving Bryce's right arm toward his left hip, causing shoulder pressure for the submission.

3 Another option is to go for an Omoplata, or shoulder lock, as Jean Jacques does here by spinning his hips to his right while throwing his right leg around Bryce's left arm.

4 Jean Jacques crosses his legs in a figure-four, left leg over right foot, and holds Bryce's belt so he can't roll forward. Jean Jacques applies the pressure by moving his hips forward.

Open guard to shoulder lock

Generally the defender in the open guard controls one of his opponent's arms with his hand, while putting one foot on the opponent's hip and the other on his biceps. The open guard offers a number of options for sweeps and submissions, however, in the yin-and-yang world of Brazilian jiu-jitsu, opportunities for attacks and sweeps are also vulnerabilities to counterattacks, in this case a guard pass. Because of that possibility, when using the open guard you need to remain very active so your opponent can't find any opportunity to pass and achieve side control. So once you open your guard, you should look for sweeps and submissions to keep your opponent always one step behind. In this technique, Jean Jacques starts with a sweep attempt and then switches to a shoulder lock.

1 Jean Jacques has Bryce in his open guard. He is holding Bryce's right sleeve with both hands to control that arm. He also has his right foot on Bryce's left biceps and his left foot pushing Bryce's right hip.

2 Jean Jacques lets go of Bryce's sleeve with his left hand, places it on the mat, and uses it to help himself sit up.

56

3 Jean Jacques throws his right leg all the way over Bryce's head.

4 Jean Jacques winds up kneeling on the ground with his right knee and head touching the mat. Notice that this whole time he is still dominating Bryce's right arm with his right hand. At this point Bryce believes that Jean Jacques is going for a sweep to his right.

5 Using his head as a pivot point, Jean Jacques pushes off his right foot and rolls forward.

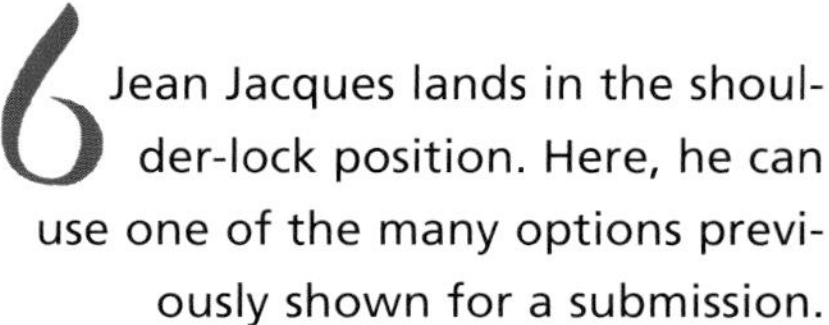

6 Jean Jacques lands in the shoulder-lock position. Here, he can use one of the many options previously shown for a submission.

Sitting guard windmill sweep

A great way to sweep from the sitting guard is the windmill sweep, because of the leverage it creates. By taking advantage of your opponent's attempt to pass, you can grab his right arm while trapping his left one with the crease behind your right knee and go for the sweep.

1 Jean Jacques is in the sitting guard with his right leg forward. He controls Bryce's right arm with his right hand and has his left arm extended back, using it as a brace to move his hips. Bryce is attempting to pass the guard to his own left by grabbing Jean Jacques's right leg.

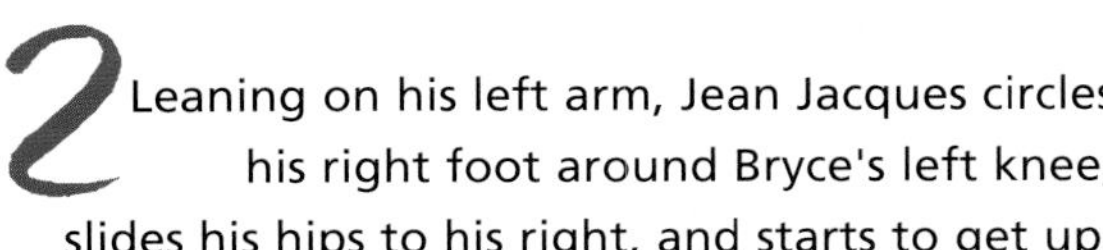

2 Leaning on his left arm, Jean Jacques circles his right foot around Bryce's left knee, slides his hips to his right, and starts to get up.

3 Again pushing off his left hand, Jean Jacques rolls forward over his right shoulder and traps Bryce's left arm by closing his right leg around it.

4 As he continues to roll, Jean Jacques pulls Bryce's right arm in, helping him roll over as well.

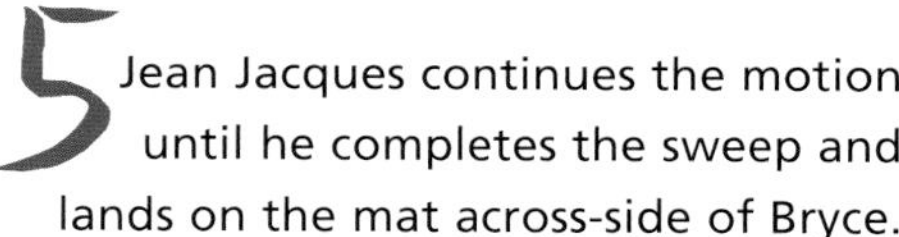

5 Jean Jacques continues the motion until he completes the sweep and lands on the mat across-side of Bryce.

6 Jean Jacques switches his hips and secures the across-side control.

Sitting guard trip sweep

This sweep is quite a modern move. It is used by the top fighters around the world against the Toreana guard pass. In the Toreana, you use your hands to hold each of your opponent's knees and then pull the knees off to one side, step around the legs, and take the side, ready for side control. You can also push his knees down while applying your weight to lock his legs in place on the ground and step around them. The key to this move is to slide your hip to the side of your opponent while pulling him forward by the collar and tripping him. This should be done when he is beginning to make his move, as his weight is already going forward. A little pull gets quite a fall because of this and your opponent usually goes down hard. Brutal and fun! When done quickly and correctly, the opponent will invariably fall face-first and be swept or taken from the back.

1 Jean Jacques is using the sitting guard and Bryce attempts to pass it with a Toreana pass.

2 As soon as he sees Bryce's attempt to pass, Jean Jacques slides his body to his left with the help of his left arm on the mat and pulls Bryce forward by the collar. Notice that since Bryce was using Jean Jacques's knees in front of him as a balancing point, he loses his balance and falls forward.

3 Jean Jacques blocks Bryce's left leg with his right foot, tripping Bryce as he continues to pull Bryce forward by the collar. Since Bryce can't step forward to catch his balance, and has nothing in front of him to hold on to, he falls.

4 Jean Jacques continues the motion by coming to the top of Bryce. He holds Bryce's right leg with his left arm.

5 Jean Jacques drives his chest forward on Bryce's, flattening him down and completing the sweep.

Sitting guard double-spin sweep

Here is another sweep from the sitting guard. Once again the opponent is attempting to pass the guard standing up, this time with a different pass. The key to this move is once again to slide your hip to the side of your opponent while holding his leg. Hip movement is one of the most important things to perfect in jiu-jitsu, especially for sweeps and reversals. If you attempt to sweep someone without escaping the hips, you will simply pull him on top of you. Notice that this time Jean Jacques maintains his right foot inside his opponent's leg and uses it as a hook for the sweep.

1 Jean Jacques is using the sitting guard to stop Bryce from passing it. Notice his feet are inside Bryce's feet and will be used as hooks to stop any passing attempt. Bryce, however, achieves an advantageous position by standing up, shifting his body to the left, and controlling Jean Jacques's gi behind the head and on the left leg. If Jean Jacques doesn't adjust, Bryce will simply spin him around to the left and achieve the guard pass.

2 Pushing off his left foot, Jean Jacques shifts his hips to the right, releases his right hand (which was blocking Bryce's left knee) and uses it to grab Bryce's left leg around the knee. Contrary to position 58, Jean Jacques keeps his right foot inside Bryce's leg and hooks it around the shin.

3 Jean Jacques spins to his left, throwing his head between Bryce's legs. Because Bryce is holding on to Jean Jacques's left knee with his hand, Jean Jacques's spinning causes Bryce to lose his balance. If Bryce doesn't release his grip on Jean Jacques's leg, he will be swept completely.

4 In this case, however, Bryce reacts quickly and properly, letting go of the grip and using his right hand to brace his fall. Jean Jacques grabs Bryce's right ankle with his left hand. Note that he maintains the hook and grab on Bryce's left leg.

5 Jean Jacques shoots his left leg through, past the right one on the mat, and switches his hips while bringing his arms together, forcing Bryce's legs together at the knee and finishing the takedown.

6 Pushing off his right foot, Jean Jacques finishes the sweep by bringing himself forward and over Bryce.

Open guard sweep to knee bar

This advanced position is one of Jean Jacques's favorites. He uses it constantly, with minor grip adjustments, in both gi and no-gi situations, resulting in either a sweep or a sweep-to-knee-bar. It is also a good way to go for the Omoplata if your opponent allows you to control his left arm more and open it.

1 Jean Jacques is using the open guard with both feet on Bryce's hips and holds Bryce's sleeves with his hands.

2 Jean Jacques pushes off his left foot and moves his hips to the right. He continues to control both sleeves as he circles his right foot and hooks it over Bryce's left arm.

3 Jean Jacques lets go of Bryce's right hand and props himself forward and up.

4 Jean Jacques pulls his left leg around until his knee is touching the mat. He now has his left elbow and knee to brace with. Notice that Jean Jacques left his right foot planted on the mat between Bryce's legs, which is important to set up the knee bar.

5 Jean Jacques does a somersault over his left shoulder, bringing Bryce with him. Notice that Bryce's left arm is completely trapped by Jean Jacques. As he rolls, Jean Jacques's right leg will hook Bryce's left, helping bring him over.

6&7 Still holding on to Bryce's left sleeve, Jean Jacques continues the roll forward and grabs Bryce's left leg with his left arm. Note Jean Jacques's leg position: his right one is over Bryce's left leg with his right foot hooking behind Bryce's right leg, while his left one is on the outside.

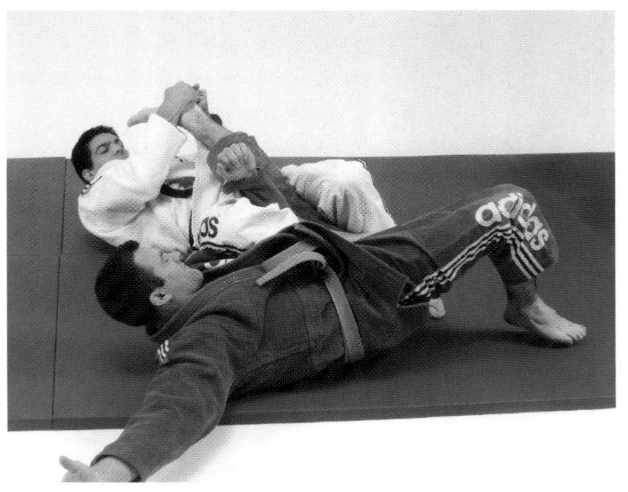

8 As they complete the roll, Jean Jacques lets go of the sleeve grip and uses both hands to pull on Bryce's left knee for a knee bar as he closes his legs to prevent any escape.

Open guard to arm lock

The arm lock is a great submission for the open guard. As the opponent attempts to pass your guard—in this case, with his right arm under the leg while dominating the right leg with his left hand—he has the option of passing to the right under your leg if you don't defend that side, or continuing to pass to his left over your right leg.

1 Jean Jacques has Kid in his guard. Kid has his right arm under Jean Jacques's left leg and is holding Jean Jacques's gi with that hand, simultaneously controlling Jean Jacques's right leg with his left hand. For his part, Jean Jacques is blocking Kid's left hand with his own right hand to prevent Kid from reaching high on Jean Jacques's collar to help his control and position. Jean Jacques is also holding Kid's right elbow with his left hand.

2 Jean Jacques quickly releases his grips and, pushing off his right forearm, he sits up and slides his hips to his left. At the same time, he pushes Kid's head across with the palm of his left hand.

3 Jean Jacques continues to get on top of Kid with his chest on Kid's back.

Detail

Notice in this reverse angle that Kid's right arm wound up trapped by Jean Jacques's right leg during the hip switch as Jean Jacques used his left leg to push Kid's arm down into his right leg.

4 Jean Jacques reaches with his left hand and grabs Kid's gi, opening his right arm and stretching his body for the arm lock.

Open guard to crucifix choke

This crucifix choke starts from the same situation as position 61. Jean Jacques once again slides his hips and pushes his opponent's head, but this time, instead of going for the arm lock, he opts for the crucifix choke. This is a good move if your opponent manages to spin his right arm and get his wrist forward to defend the arm lock.

1 Jean Jacques begins as he did in position 61, step 2.

2 Jean Jacques sits up and goes on top of Kid's back.

3 Jean Jacques traps Kid's right arm with his legs, much as in the previous technique. This time, however, Kid defends his arm by twisting the wrist.

4 Jean Jacques crosses his feet and rolls forward over his left shoulder, carrying Kid with him.

5 As he continues to roll, Jean Jacques is already preparing his right hand to go for the choke.

6 When he lands on his back, Jean Jacques reaches around Kid's neck, grabs the opposite collar with his right hand, and pulls it across for the choke. Notice that Kid is completely in the crucifix position, with his arms trapped by Jean Jacques's legs and left arm.

Sitting guard sweep to leg lock

Today's modern jiu-jitsu fighters are constantly using the stand-up cross-knee guard pass to overcome their opponents' guards. This powerful guard pass must be intercepted early to be successfully defended. Fighters faced with that problem have developed a few counters to the stand-up cross-knee pass. One of the most effective is to sit up and wrap the passer's leg. Jean Jacques here demonstrates not only the proper defense but goes a few steps further and does a sweep to a leg lock.

1 Kid attempts a stand-up cross-knee guard pass. Notice that he is holding Jean Jacques's gi behind the head with his right hand and Jean Jacques's right leg with his left. He also has his right leg positioned between Jean Jacques's legs, ready to cross the knee. His next step, if not properly defended, would be to drive Jean Jacques back to the mat, slip his right arm inside Jean Jacques's left armpit, cross his right knee over Jean Jacques's hips, and drive his weight forward. Sensing an imminent guard pass, Jean Jacques immediately sits up, wraps Kid's right leg with his left arm, and scoots his hips to his left. He also grabs Kid's left wrist with his right hand.

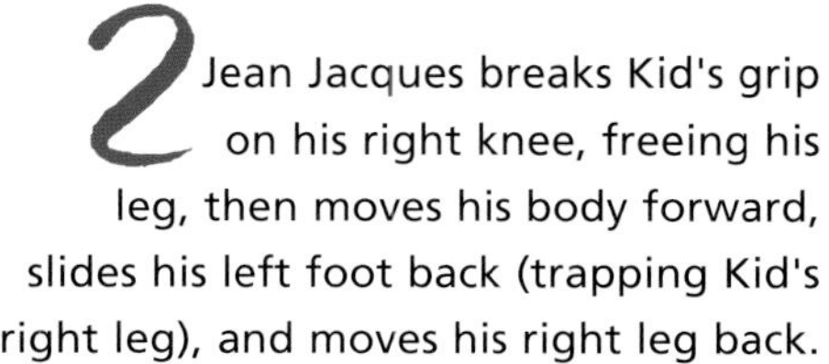

2 Jean Jacques breaks Kid's grip on his right knee, freeing his leg, then moves his body forward, slides his left foot back (trapping Kid's right leg), and moves his right leg back.

3 Jean Jacques continues to slide his right leg back and presses his torso forward on Kid's right knee. Since Kid's right leg is trapped by Jean Jacques's left leg, the pressure forces him down.

4 Jean Jacques continues to move forward as he locks Kid's right foot in the crease of his left leg. Notice that throughout this sequence he is still holding on to Kid's left arm so Kid can't spin away and escape.

5 Jean Jacques locks a figure-four with his legs, right leg around the left foot, trapping Kid's right leg, and sets the leg lock by pushing his hips down on the knee.

Sitting guard sweep: opponent counters

The previous technique involved sweeping your opponent back, but sometimes a cagey opponent faced with you sitting and grabbing his leg will immediately press forward with his right knee to defend the sweep. In that case, or if your opponent remains in a neutral stance, you can use this sweep variation.

1 As in position 63, step 1, Jean Jacques sits up and controls Kid's right leg. Kid, sensing the possibility of a sweep, can either force his right knee forward onto Jean Jacques's chest or, as in this case, remain in a neutral stance in good base. So Jean Jacques places his right foot on top of Kid's left foot, preventing it from moving forward.

2 Jean Jacques changes his grip on Kid's left arm by passing it from his right hand to his left and uses his right hand to grip Kid's collar.

3 Jean Jacques starts the sweep by throwing his head toward the right, in the direction of the mat, as he pulls down on Kid's gi. With Jean Jacques controlling his left side, Kid cannot step forward with his left foot or brace with his left arm, and has no choice but to fall.

4 Jean Jacques continues the rotation and goes up on Kid, completing the sweep.

Butterfly guard sweep with guard pass

This variation of the regular butterfly guard sweep is useful when an opponent is able to stretch his left leg and brace against the original sweep.

1 Jean Jacques attempts a butterfly guard sweep. He traps Kid's right arm with his left one and has his left foot hooked onto Kid's right leg. Jean Jacques begins the motion by throwing his head to the right toward the mat while lifting his left leg.

2 Kid blocks the sweep by extending his left leg as a brace.

3 Jean Jacques changes his right-hand grip from Kid's sleeve, grabs Kid's left ankle, and pulls it forward, causing Kid to fall back.

4 Jean Jacques continues to pull the ankle and moves forward on top of Kid.

5 Jean Jacques begins to pass the guard by crossing his left knee in front of Kid's hips until it touches the mat. Notice that Jean Jacques is leaning forward, applying his weight on that knee, and is pulling up on Kid's left arm with his right arm, adding a lot of pressure to Kid's torso. He keeps his left foot over Kid's leg as a hook to keep Kid from closing his legs and achieving the half guard.

6 Jean Jacques steps over with his right leg and then releases his left foot hook as he drives his left knee forward and completes the pass.

Half-guard sweep to cross-knee pass

The half guard is perhaps the position that has developed the most in modern Brazilian jiu-jitsu. Once thought of as merely a stage between the full guard and being passed, the modern half guard has become a breeding ground for innovative sweeps and submissions. Jean Jacques loves the half guard and uses it to develop several variations. As he says, "The key to the half guard is not one specific position or foot placement but rather a creative thinking that starts with positioning yourself under your opponent." Here, Jean Jacques parlays one of his favorite sweeps into a cross-knee pass.

1 Jean Jacques has Kid in the half guard. Kid attempted a standing guard pass and Jean Jacques quickly adjusted himself to the half guard. As he stated above, he positions himself under Kid, his left leg hooked under Kid's left leg and both hands grabbing Kid's sleeves.

2 Jean Jacques traps Kid's left foot with his right leg, scooting his hips to the left as he pulls down on Kid's left sleeve and lifts up on the right one. He also points his left knee forward, forcing Kid to fall to Jean Jacques's right.

3 Jean Jacques continues the motion as he comes up on the falling Kid.

4 As Kid's back hits the mat, Jean Jacques pulls up on both sleeves and drives his left knee forward. Notice Jean Jacques's posture with his back straight and his hips forward.

5 Jean Jacques continues to drive his left knee forward, opens his right leg and, pushing off his toes, applies the weight of his torso to Kid's chest. The pressure will be too much and Kid will allow the pass.

Half-guard sweep to guard pass

As in position 66, Jean Jacques starts by attempting a sweep, but here his opponent leans to his right, defending it. Jean Jacques then switches to a different half-guard sweep, hoping to throw the opponent over his head. Again the opponent defends by getting in base, putting his weight down on his hips. Jean Jacques must proceed to a third option, sweeping him back, and lands with his hands in perfect position for a guard pass.

1 Jean Jacques attempts the sweep shown in position 66, but Kid shifts his weight to his right and defends it. Notice again Jean Jacques's left leg and knee placement and his right leg blocking Kid's left foot.

2 Jean Jacques pulls Kid up toward his head by the arm and leg hooks. Sensing a sweep forward, Kid steps out with his right leg.

3 Jean Jacques reaches with his left arm inside Kid's right leg, placing his own body completely under Kid. Kid still feels threatened by the forward sweep and defends it by lowering his hips, weighing down on Jean Jacques's left leg. Had Kid not reacted this way, Jean Jacques would have simply continued to sweep him over his head by pulling Kid's left arm down and kicking his own left leg, forcing Kid to fall forward over his own left shoulder.

4 With the forward sweep well defended, Jean Jacques reverses everything. He turns his body to his left and gets up on Kid, pulling him down. The weight of Kid's body leaning back helps him fall.

5 As Kid's back starts to hit the mat, Jean Jacques lets go of his right-hand grip on Kid's sleeve and slides his arm under Kid's left leg. Note that his left arm was already wrapped around Kid's right leg.

6 Jean Jacques finishes with his arms under Kid's legs, in perfect position for a guard pass.

Half-guard sweep: opponent wraps arm

Quite often in half-guard pass/defense exchanges you will get your opponent in your half guard and be able to slide your right arm under his left one, giving you a clear path to slide to his back. The proper defense is for the opponent to wrap his left arm over and inside your right arm, preventing you from going to the back. Here, Jean Jacques demonstrates how to take advantage of this and complete the pass.

1 Jean Jacques has Kid in his half guard and is able to slide his right arm under Kid's left one, giving him a clear path to slide to Kid's back.

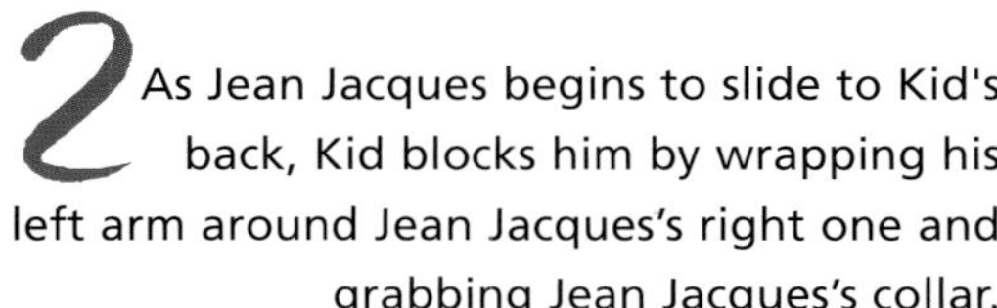

2 As Jean Jacques begins to slide to Kid's back, Kid blocks him by wrapping his left arm around Jean Jacques's right one and grabbing Jean Jacques's collar.

3 Jean Jacques removes his right arm from under Kid's armpit and locks it over Kid's left arm, grabbing Kid's left wrist as well. At this point Kid's left arm is completely trapped under Jean Jacques's right armpit.

4 Jean Jacques lays back, pulling Kid forward, and with his left hand grabs Kid's right pant leg around the knee.

5 Jean Jacques uses his momentum and continues the motion by rotating his body to his right. He brings Kid with him by the trapped left arm and by lifting Kid's right leg with his left arm.

6 As Kid's back is about to hit the mat, Jean Jacques steps around with his left leg to complete the pass.

Half-guard sweep: opponent slides arm under leg

This time the opponent attempts to pass the guard with his arm under Jean Jacques's leg. Jean Jacques is able to secure the half guard and needs to do something to prevent his opponent from simply continuing to the pass, as he has a solid position to pass the guard. An opponent in this position may hold the belt to control the hips or simply hold the gi skirt.

1 Kid is in the half guard with his left arm under Jean Jacques's leg and his left leg trapped. Jean Jacques puts his right foot on the mat and scoots his hips to his right, making sure he retains his left foot over Kid's left leg to keep him from passing. He then reaches with his right hand and holds Kid's left wrist.

2 Jean Jacques yanks up on Kid's sleeve, causing him to lean forward. This also helps Jean Jacques to lock his legs around Kid's left leg. Notice that at this point Jean Jacques has completely dominated the left side of his opponent.

3 Jean Jacques places both feet on the mat and pushes off to a bridge. He shifts his torso to his left and pulls Kid's left arm as he uses his left-hand grip on Kid's right arm to twist him, causing him to fall to Jean Jacques's right. Notice that by planting both feet on the mat, Jean Jacques maintains the block on his opponent's left leg.

4 As Kid starts to fall to the mat, Jean Jacques plants his right hand down and uses it to bring himself up and over Kid.

5 Jean Jacques continues the motion to get on top and ends up in Kid's half guard when he completes the sweep.

Sitting guard push sweep

This very clever sweep from the sitting guard occurs frequently when defending the pass, as sometimes the opponent disengages himself and stands up in front of you. The effectiveness of this move is based on its simplicity and the surprise factor.

1 Jean Jacques is in his sitting guard, with Kid standing in front of him attempting to pass the guard. At this point neither adversary has a grip on the other.

2 Jean Jacques puts his left foot and right hand down on the mat and uses them to lift his body and scoot forward toward Kid, placing his legs between Kid's legs.

3 Jean Jacques hooks his feet behind Kid's ankles and pushes with both hands on Kid's thighs.

4 Since he cannot move his feet, Kid falls backward.

5 As Kid lands on the ground, Jean Jacques completes the sweep by coming over the top.

Half-guard helicopter sweep

This is a very complex move that should be used only after you have mastered it by practicing it many times. It is highly effective, but risky, as you may expose your leg to a knee lock if not properly executed.

1 Jean Jacques has Kid in his half guard. His right leg is around Kid's left leg and his foot is hooked on Kid's hip. Jean Jacques's right hand is blocking Kid's left ankle and his left hand is holding Kid's left sleeve.

2 Jean Jacques pushes off his left leg and rotates his body to the right, pulling on Kid's sleeve at the same time. He reaches with his right hand to grab Kid's right ankle. Make sure you don't extend your right leg, as you risk the chance of a knee lock if you miss the grip on your opponent's ankle.

3 Once he has secured a grip on Kid's right gi pants or ankle, Jean Jacques continues the rotation by bringing his head toward Kid's ankle. At this point he extends his right leg between Kid's legs without fearing a knee lock and pulls Kid's sleeve toward his left, causing Kid's body to spin counterclockwise.

4 Jean Jacques kicks his right leg over and lifts Kid's right ankle, causing him to fall.

5 Jean Jacques continues the rotation to get on top of Kid, making sure he doesn't let go of any grips.

6 Once Kid has his back on the mat, Jean Jacques slips his body between Kid's legs.

7 Jean Jacques completes the sweep, ending up in Kid's half guard.

Guard pass: shortcut to the mount

Jean Jacques likes to cut to the chase, so when the opportunity presents itself, he will take a shortcut. Here, he demonstrates a very effective way to pass the guard directly to the mount. The opponent has Jean Jacques in his open guard, in this case with a De La Riva hook with his right foot, but this technique will also work when the opponent has both feet inside as hooks.

1 Jean Jacques is in Kid's guard with his left leg hooked. Notice that Jean Jacques is holding Kid's gi pants with his right hand to retain control of his own right arm, otherwise Kid would be able to pull it at will.

2 Jean Jacques steps back with his right leg and pushes down on Kid's right leg with his right hand, placing it between his own legs. By doing that he releases the pressure applied by Kid's left leg against his hips.

3 In a sudden move, Jean Jacques pulls himself down with his left hand and throws his hips forward and down on top of Kid, sliding his left knee over Kid's right thigh. Kid had no way to block this since Jean Jacques's left knee was already in place and his right leg was free.

4 Jean Jacques continues to drive his knees forward, until his feet are on the mat, and quickly achieves the mounted position.

Guard pass: traditional, with change of direction

One of the worst things you can do, in jiu-jitsu and in life, is to be single-minded, stuck on one way of doing something. This makes you predictable and easy to defeat. Always be creative and flexible and find new ways to achieve your goal. Here, Jean Jacques is passing the guard in one of the most traditional ways, pulling himself under his opponent's right leg, but his opponent blocks the pass. Rather than trying to force his position, Jean Jacques changes direction.

1 Jean Jacques is passing the guard with his left arm under Kid's right leg, holding Kid's gi, and his right hand controlling Kid's left knee, pushing it down on the mat.

2 As Jean Jacques starts to pass to his left, Kid blocks his hips and shoulder with both arms.

3 Rather than fighting the block and trying to force the pass to the left, Jean Jacques quickly releases his right-hand grip on the knee and reverses the field, circling his body to his right.

4 Jean Jacques continues to circle around to his right as he leads with a right-arm swing and drops his right knee to the mat over Kid's left leg. Notice that Jean Jacques left his right foot hooked over Kid's left leg to prevent the half guard.

5 Jean Jacques continues the motion and, as soon as his right elbow reaches the mat next to Kid's head, Jean Jacques swings his left leg around, switching his hips. Once he has secured side control, he releases his right foot hook on Kid's leg.

Star guard pass

Here Jean Jacques demonstrates one of the star passes. In this case, he is passing the guard on the ground and his opponent uses a right-foot hook to attempt a sweep or simply to block the pass. The guard passes are most effective when done without much setup, or with a disguise in the setup, to surprise your opponent. If he senses you are preparing too much, he will react and defend it. Be discreet and only apply your weight at the last minute before you go up.

1 Jean Jacques is using one of the many ways to pass the guard, controlling Kid's hips with his left arm, holding the belt and keeping his elbow close to the body. He also has his right knee over Kid's leg with his right foot hooking the left leg.

2 Jean Jacques continues the pass by pushing down on Kid's left leg with his right hand and switching his left foot to trap it. At this point, Kid decides to place his right foot as a hook under Jean Jacques's left leg to defend the pass.

3 Jean Jacques puts his head on the mat right next to Kid's armpit, braces with both hands, and springs his body straight up.

4 With his legs in the air, Jean Jacques spins his body to his left. Note that his right hand still controls Kid's left knee and his head and left arm lock Kid's torso, preventing him from moving.

5 Jean Jacques lands across-side and completes the star pass.

Guard pass: traditional, with change of direction and hip switch

Like position 73, this is a variation of the traditional guard pass. Instead of going to his left, Jean Jacques is again forced to change directions and come back to the center, but this time the opponent blocks his attempt to pass his right knee through the middle. In this case, Jean Jacques must switch his hips and deflect the opponent's block.

1 As in position 73, Jean Jacques was passing the guard around Kid's right leg, but was forced to change direction. His first step is to kneel over Kid's left leg with his right one, making sure to leave his right foot hooked over Kid's leg to prevent Kid from trapping Jean Jacques's leg for a half guard.

2 Kid, however, blocks Jean Jacques's right knee, preventing the pass. Rather than fight the block, Jean Jacques switches his hips as he drives forward onto Kid by pulling Kid's gi collar, sliding his left knee over Kid's left leg, again leaving his foot hooked on it.

3 Jean Jacques grabs Kid's left sleeve and pulls up on it. He drives his body forward to the left, pushing Kid's right leg and driving Kid's knee to his own head.

4 Jean Jacques releases his right foot and steps over Kid's leg, and then repeats the motion with his left foot to get across-side. Alternatively, after stepping over with his right leg, Jean Jacques could just continue to drive his left knee forward until his left foot slid over Kid's leg. He would achieve side control just the same, but his hips would be facing Kid's head instead of being square with Kid's body.

Across-side to mount to arm lock

This is one of the most ingenious ways to achieve the mount. Jean Jacques then takes it one step further to get an arm lock.

1 Jean Jacques is across-side with his hips facing Kid. His first step is to attack Kid's left arm, as if he is going for a key lock. He uses his right arm to push down on the arm as he tries to pry it away from Kid's chest. Sensing this, Kid resists by pulling his arm to his chest even harder.

2 Jean Jacques continues to force the arm down and uses it to brace and lift his body up as he throws his left leg over Kid's head.

3 Once his leg clears Kid's head, Jean Jacques brings it down right over Kid's shoulder.

4 Jean Jacques could easily attain the mounted position by kneeling on the ground, but instead he goes for the submission. With his right arm, he pulls up on Kid's left arm as he leans to his left until the arm is straight.

5 Jean Jacques passes his right leg over Kid's head, applying the arm lock with his hips.

Mounted position to triangle

Want to try some subterfuge? This attack from the mounted position involves baiting your opponent by pretending to miss an arm lock attack and instead going for a triangle choke.

1 Jean Jacques is mounted on Kid. He starts to attack Kid's right arm for a key lock by pushing it down with his arms. Kid defends by pushing up against the force.

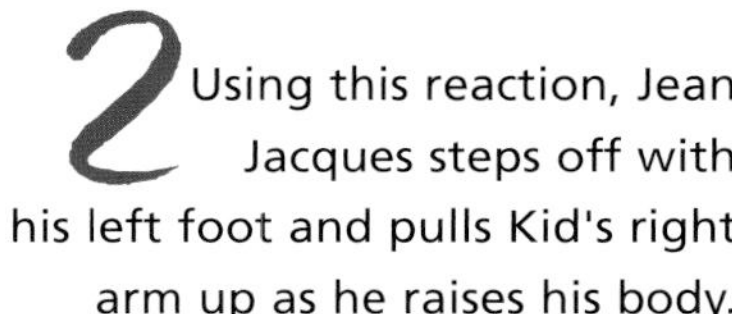

2 Using this reaction, Jean Jacques steps off with his left foot and pulls Kid's right arm up as he raises his body.

3 Jean Jacques rotates his body to his right and throws his right leg around, as if he was going for an arm lock, except that he is seemingly attacking the wrong arm.

4 Kid naturally turns over to defend the arm lock and to get on top.

5 Jean Jacques opens his right leg, allowing Kid's head to come through.

6 Jean Jacques pulls Kid's arm in and locks his legs in a figure-four, right leg bent over the shoulder and under Jean Jacques's own left foot, locking Kid's head and arm in the triangle choke.

Mounted position to Omoplata

This picks up at position 77, step 5. As Jean Jacques falls back, allowing his opponent to come over, he goes for an Omoplata, instead of the triangle choke, because the position of his opponent's head doesn't lend itself to the triangle.

1 Jean Jacques has opted out of the mount, as in the previous position, and has fallen to the mat, allowing Kid to come up. Jean Jacques could go for a triangle choke from here, but decides not to because Kid's head is pressed down on Jean Jacques's leg, preventing Jean Jacques from having good access for a triangle choke.

2 Instead of allowing Kid to come up in between his legs, Jean Jacques throws his left leg over Kid's back, blocking it, while keeping his right foot on the mat.

3 Pushing off his right foot, Jean Jacques pivots his body to his left. He moves Kid's arm to Kid's hips, crosses his left leg over Kid's back around the right arm, and locks his left foot under his right leg.

4 Pushing off his right arm, Jean Jacques sits up and applies the shoulder lock.

Mounted position to arm lock: distraction technique

It is very common for a mounted defender to have his arms bent and held tightly against his chest to prevent a key lock, as shown here. The elbows close to the body block you from hiking up with your legs to reach a high mounted position. Here, Jean Jacques uses the defender's collar to pry his arm open and then reacts to the proper defense by attacking the opposite arm. This same attack works when the defender holds his own collar to prevent you from applying a choke.

1 Jean Jacques is mounted on Kid, who has proper posture, elbows close to his body and arms bent and tight against his chest, to prevent Jean Jacques from hiking up. Jean Jacques opens Kid's right gi lapel with both hands.

2 Jean Jacques loops it over Kid's right arm and pushes it down with the weight of his body. This causes Kid's arm to open for the key lock, as he cannot resist the weight of Jean Jacques's body.

3 Sensing the key-lock attack, the intelligent opponent will turn to his right and use his left hand to grab your right wrist to prevent it, as Kid does here. If he fails to do this, you can simply apply the key lock to the right arm.

4 Jean Jacques pivots his body making sure he pushes his hips against Kid's right shoulder to prevent him from turning back and yanking his right arm out.

5 As he swings his leg over Kid's head, Jean Jacques lets go of Kid's collar and grabs Kid's left arm instead as he falls to the mat for the arm lock.

6 The arm lock is complete.

Across-side attack 1: knee bar

Baiting the opponent again, Jean Jacques starts this attack by sliding his knee over his opponent's stomach, as if he was going for the mount or a reverse knee-on-stomach attack, and reacts to the opponent's defense by taking the knee bar.

1 Jean Jacques is across-side on Kid with his hips facing away from Kid's head. Kid has his left foot on his right knee to block the mount.

2 Jean Jacques pushes off his left foot and begins to slide his right knee over Kid's stomach, close to the left thigh, while he pulls Kid's right arm for extra control.

3 Quickly, Jean Jacques lets go of his left-hand grip on Kid's right arm and grabs Kid's left leg instead.

4 Jean Jacques falls back for the knee bar. Note that Jean Jacques still has his right knee over Kid's hip, trapping his left leg.

Across-side attack 2: toe hold

Back when jiu-jitsu practitioners and competition rules discouraged foot and leg attacks, Jean Jacques was still practicing them. Now that the sport has opened up to these submissions, Jean Jacques uses them in competition as well. Here, Jean Jacques demonstrates a very effective and sneaky attack from across-side.

1 Jean Jacques is across-side on Kid. Kid has his leg up, right foot on his left knee, to block Jean Jacques from attaining the mounted position.

2 Jean Jacques raises his body quickly and attacks Kid's right foot with a toe hold, his left hand holding Kid's toes while his right hand wraps around Kid's calf until it locks onto his own left wrist.

3 Jean Jacques steps over Kid with his left leg.

4 Jean Jacques continues to fall to his left as he applies pressure on Kid's foot. Kid turns to his own left to relieve some of the pressure.

5 Jean Jacques continues to turn, following Kid until he taps from the pressure.

Knee-on-stomach to arm lock

The knee-on-stomach is a dynamic position that opens up a variety of attacks. In this case, Jean Jacques begins by attacking his opponent's neck for a choke and reacts to the escape by changing to an arm lock.

1 Jean Jacques has proper knee-on-stomach posture. Notice his knee on Flavio's stomach and his right leg open out for balance, while his left hand holds Flavio's belt and his right hand controls Flavio's left sleeve. Flavio is attempting to escape the position by pushing Jean Jacques's knee with his right hand.

2 Sensing that Flavio's attention is directed to the escape in the knee area, Jean Jacques begins to attack Flavio's neck. He leans forward, pulling Flavio's left arm, and reaches with his left hand deep inside Flavio's collar for the choke. Flavio is still preoccupied with escaping the knee-on-stomach, but makes an attempt to defend the choke with his right arm by pulling Jean Jacques's left elbow. However, he makes the mistake of leaving his elbow up away from his body, where it is vulnerable to an arm lock.

3 Jean Jacques sees the opening and takes advantage of it, spinning to his right and throwing his right leg over Flavio's head. He puts his weight on Flavio's right hand, pressing down on Flavio's right shoulder to prevent him from turning.

4 Jean Jacques falls back to the mat for the arm lock. Notice Jean Jacques's knees closing around Flavio's arm to take away any space for a possible escape.

Knee-on-stomach to choke 1

Diverging from the previous position, this time as Jean Jacques attacks the neck the opponent's defense is better—he keeps his left elbow close to his body. Jean Jacques must change to a choke.

1 Jean Jacques has knee-on-stomach and attacks Flavio's neck while trying to open up his arm. Flavio defends the choke with his left arm, grabbing Jean Jacques's forearm and keeping his own left elbow close to his body to avoid getting it trapped in an arm lock.

2 Jean Jacques leans back and places his right hand, palm down, into Flavio's right collar. Notice that this is opposite to the instinctive way of grabbing a collar, with the palm facing up. This is necessary to put the blade of Jean Jacques's arm on Flavio's neck, to deliver the choke when Jean Jacques pushes his elbow down to the ground.

3 Jean Jacques lowers his body and drives his forearm down and across Flavio's neck, while still pulling with his left arm for the choke. Jean Jacques adds pressure to the choke by driving his right elbow down to the mat and circling it toward Flavio's head if necessary.

Knee-on-stomach to opposite-arm arm lock

If your opponent turns into you as he attempts to escape from the knee-on-stomach position, and leaves his right elbow open, you can opt for this unusual opposite-arm arm lock.

1 Jean Jacques begins with the proper knee-on-stomach position. Flavio has both hands on Jean Jacques's knee, setting up his escape.

2 As Flavio pushes Jean Jacques's knee and turns into Jean Jacques, he leaves his right elbow open. Jean Jacques quickly slips his left arm in the opening, brings his right leg in, and plants his right arm on Flavio's right shoulder to help spin him.

3 Jean Jacques steps over Flavio with his right leg and pulls up on Flavio's elbow, to help turn Flavio over and make it a shorter route. He also holds Flavio's right knee by the pants with his right hand to keep Flavio from turning over too much. Notice how Jean Jacques's left leg is extended and his right knee is already bent close to Flavio's right armpit, making it easy to go for the arm lock. Bringing Flavio's elbow up makes Jean Jacques's job a lot easier; he can turn Flavio over on his side instead of flat on his back, making a tighter turn.

4 With his position exactly where he wants it, Jean Jacques falls back for the arm lock, left leg over Flavio's face and right shin in Flavio's right armpit. Notice that Jean Jacques is still holding on to Flavio's gi pants to keep him from turning in an attempt to escape.

Knee-on-stomach to choke 2

This variation differs from position 83 in that Jean Jacques controls the position with his right hand holding the back of Flavio's collar. He wants to go for a submission but does it without releasing his grip and risking losing control of the position. This position, though less direct, holds one significant advantage over position 83. Because your opponent's collar is not being directly attacked, he tends to feel safer in this position, and may not put his defenses into play as quickly. Before he knows it, the choke comes out of nowhere.

1 Jean Jacques starts with the knee-on-stomach while Flavio is focusing on escaping by having his hands on Jean Jacques's knee. This time Jean Jacques's right hand holds behind Flavio's collar, as opposed to position 83, where he pulled Flavio's right arm instead.

2 With Flavio's attention focused on Jean Jacques's knee, Jean Jacques attacks Flavio's right collar with his left hand, palm up.

85

3 Jean Jacques applies the choking pressure by bringing his chest down and stepping around Flavio's head with his right leg as he kneels with his left knee and brings his elbows together. Notice that Jean Jacques keeps his right arm somewhat straight to add pressure. It is a very common mistake to bend that elbow as well when applying this choke, but that will only reduce pressure, because the defender's head will rest back in the crease.

Detail

In this detail you can see the proper way to grip the collar and apply the pressure. Again, notice that Jean Jacques's right arm is not totally bent but rather fairly straight, forcing Flavio's head forward into the choke.

No-gi mount to arm lock and triangle choke

The mounted position is a highly desirable position in both jiu-jitsu and submission wrestling. Most competitions reward achieving it with great points. In sports jiu-jitsu you get 4 and in ADCC submission wrestling you get 2. One would expect that such a dominant position would have a great number of attacks, but that is not the case. Being in a precarious position, the defender usually protects himself ferociously, blocking most avenues of attacking the neck and arms. In submission wrestling, with the absence of the gi, there are even fewer options, since you cannot use the collar and sleeve chokes. There are, however, a few masters who have developed a solid arsenal of no-gi attacks. Here, Jean Jacques demonstrates both an arm lock and a triangle option that develop from the mount. The first step for an attack is to introduce some sort of chaos into the scene. Jean Jacques does that by pulling his opponent's head up with his hand.

1 Jean Jacques is mounted on Adam. Adam has his hands on each side of his throat to block possible chokes. Jean Jacques needs to create an opening and does so by pulling Adam's head up with his hand.

2 As Adam struggles with the pressure, Jean Jacques advances his left knee by sliding it under Adam's right elbow, exposing Adam's arm.

3 Bracing off his left arm, Jean Jacques shifts his body to the left and slips his right leg over Adam's left elbow.

4 Jean Jacques continues placing his right leg behind Adam's head, now using both hands to pull Adam's head up. Notice that at this point, Adam's right arm and head are trapped inside Jean Jacques's legs.

5 Jean Jacques shifts his weight to his right knee, lifts his hips, and completes the arm lock. Notice that Jean Jacques has both hands dominating Adam's right arm and both elbows close to his body for extra leverage. He applies the pressure by pushing his hips forward while arching his torso.

6 As an option, in case Adam slips his arm out of the grip or had tucked it earlier, Jean Jacques grabs his right shin with his left hand, pushes off his left foot, and rolls to his right.

7 As he completes the roll, Jean Jacques closes his legs in a figure-four, left leg over right foot, and applies the triangle choke.

No-gi across-side to head-and-arm choke

The across-side position offers a great variety of attacks in both sports jiu-jitsu and submission wrestling. In no-gi situations it is preferable to the mounted position because it is much more stable and easier to control. Here, Jean Jacques demonstrates a solid and effective choke from across-side.

1 Jean Jacques has side control on Adam. His right arm is under Adam's head and his right shoulder pushes Adam's chin, preventing him from turning to his left and attempting to replace the guard. Adam uses his right forearm on Jean Jacques's throat to create space and keep some distance for a possible escape.

2 Jean Jacques releases the pressure of his grip around Adam's chest, lifts his head, and pushes Adam's elbow up with his left hand.

3 Jean Jacques quickly brings his head down, trapping Adam's arm with it. This is the critical moment in this technique; if Jean Jacques doesn't gets his head quickly down and around Adam's elbow, he won't be able to trap it.

4 Jean Jacques cinches the lock on Adam's head and arm by pushing his body forward. He switches his hips and slides his right knee over Adam's stomach. With his left hand, he blocks Adam's right leg.

5 Jean Jacques loops his left leg over and gets to the opposite side of Adam. Notice Jean Jacques's base with his left leg and arm.

6 Jean Jacques closes the choke by grabbing his left biceps with his right hand and placing his left hand behind his head. He will apply the choking pressure by pushing off his left leg as he presses forward and down with his head against Adam's arm and head. He adds even more pressure by bringing his elbows together.

No-gi across-side to arm lock

In this variation of the traditional arm lock from across-side, Jean Jacques utilizes a unique setup to control his opponent and attacks the arm that is closer to him, rather than the opposite arm, which is more common.

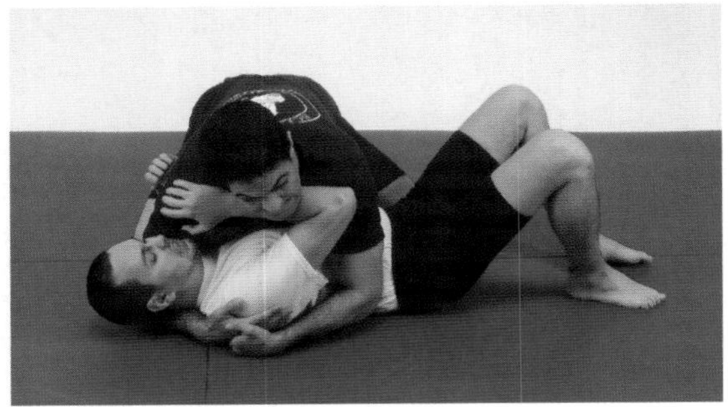

1 Jean Jacques is across-side on Adam. Notice that Jean Jacques has normal control, with his right arm wrapped around Adam's neck as he pushes his right shoulder into Adam's chin, forcing Adam to remain flat on the ground. Again, Adam has his right forearm on Jean Jacques's throat to create space for a possible escape and his left forearm blocking Jean Jacques's hips for extra space and to prevent the mount.

2 The forearm brace on the throat can be a very difficult obstacle to remove, as Adam has tremendous leverage there. Instead of trying to overpower it, Jean Jacques plants his left hand on the ground and drives his left shoulder up to Adam's head, cleverly deflecting Adam's forearm toward his head.

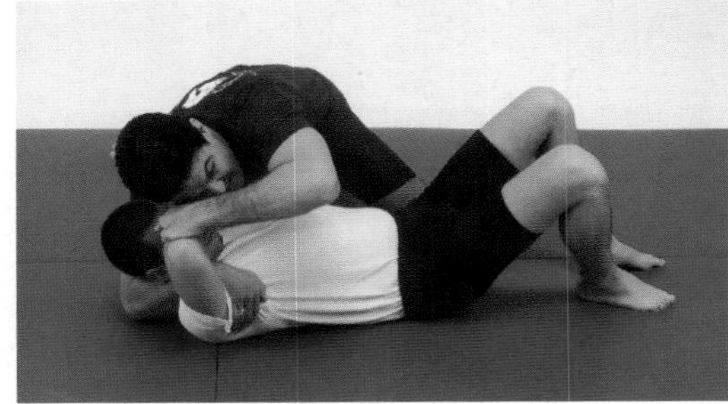

3 Jean Jacques blocks Adam's arm with his left hand and hooks his right hand in Adam's right armpit.

4 Jean Jacques raises his body and drives his right arm forward, pushing Adam's head with it. Note that this "cervical hold" is legal in some submission wrestling events, but usually illegal in sports jiu-jitsu (though often practiced anyway). It can damage the cervical spine—the seven vertebrae of the spinal column in the neck—and should be practiced with extreme caution.

5 Needless to say, the cervical hold is a very uncomfortable position for Adam, who immediately needs to release his right arm or else submit. Adam releases it by rolling to his right. Another option the defender has here is to shoot his left arm inside yours, in which case you'll need to switch to the attack shown in position 89.

6 Jean Jacques continues to press his right arm against Adam's head as he switches his hips to his right and lassoes Adam's left arm with his own left arm.

7 Jean Jacques throws his right leg over Adam's right arm, locking the arm as his foot hits the ground. Notice that Jean Jacques does not release his right-hand hook on Adam's armpit until he is sure that he has firm control with his foot. This prevents Adam from turning to his left and into Jean Jacques, which would allow him to pull his left elbow out and escape the arm lock.

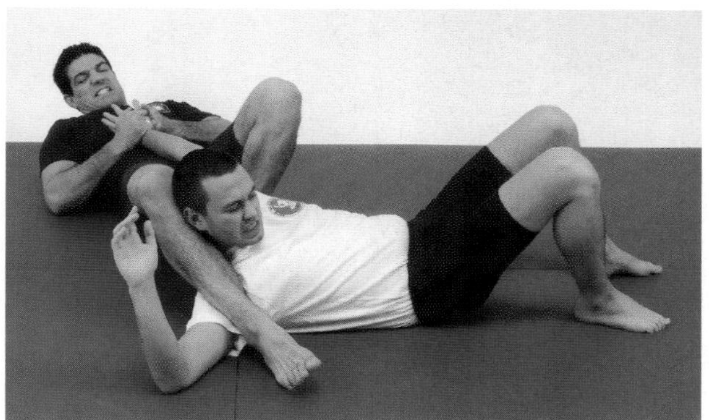

8 Once he is sure of the control over Adam's right arm, Jean Jacques releases his own right arm, grabs Adam's left arm with both hands, and falls back for the arm lock.

No-gi across-side to arm lock 2

In this variation of position 88, the opponent shoots his left arm through your left arm, instead of rolling to his right as before.

1 As in position 88, step 5, Adam removed his left arm from blocking Jean Jacques's hips to release the pressure on his neck, but this time, rather than roll to his right, he simply shot his arm inside Jean Jacques's left arm.

2 Jean Jacques wraps Adam's left arm with his own left arm and shoots his right leg forward until he plants his foot on the mat near Adam's right shoulder.

3 Jean Jacques loops his foot over Adam's right arm until he hooks it on Adam's armpit.

4 Since Jean Jacques has Adam's arm trapped between his left arm and body, it is easier for Jean Jacques to arm lock it simply by placing both hands on Adam's elbow, bringing his knees together, and leaning back to his left, causing tremendous pressure on Adam's elbow joint.

No-gi across-side to mount and choke

This position starts out much like the previous two, but this time the defender is able to turn to his right, or may be forced to his side by the attacker. Seeing this, Jean Jacques opts to mount his opponent, force him to turn over, and apply a rear choke.

1 As in positions 88 and 89, Jean Jacques is across-side on Adam, but this time Adam has turned on his side. This situation can occur if Adam was forced to his side by Jean Jacques, or if Adam attempted to escape by turning to all fours and Jean Jacques interceded. Note that Jean Jacques has his right arm wrapped around Adam's neck and is using both hands to hold Adam's left wrist.

2 Jean Jacques plants his left hand on the ground and drives his left shoulder forward, while pulling Adam's left arm across his own face, forcing Adam to turn over even more.

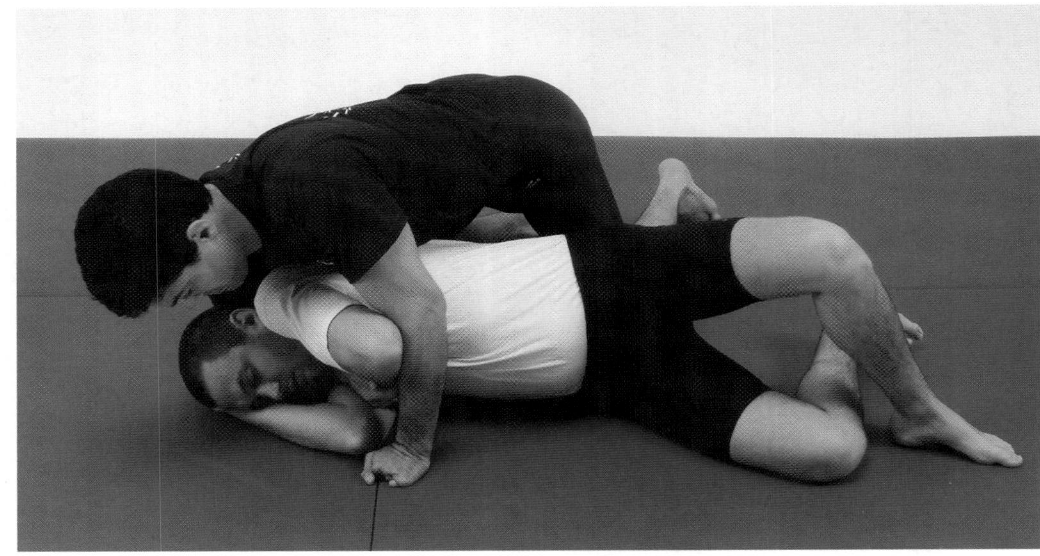

3 At this point, Jean Jacques simply loops his left leg over Adam's body and mounts him.

4 Jean Jacques continues to turn Adam over onto his stomach by pulling his left arm across.

5 Jean Jacques forces Adam flat on his stomach by driving his hips forward and down on Adam's back while his feet hook Adam's hips. Jean Jacques slides his right arm in front of Adam's neck until his hand comes out the other side. He then clasps his hands together and pulls his right forearm up and across Adam's neck for the choke.

No-gi guard pass to knee bar

Jean Jacques is attempting a guard pass to his right. His opponent, however, has Jean Jacques's left foot trapped between his legs, preventing the completion of the guard pass, and is using his arms to block Jean Jacques's hips as well. From this position, Jean Jacques can continue to try to pass by freeing his left foot, or can go for this clever submission.

1 Jean Jacques is attempting a guard pass but has his foot caught between Adam's legs.

2 Jean Jacques turns to his right and plants both hands on the mat.

3 Bracing off his arms, Jean Jacques throws his right leg over Adam's body as he continues to turn to his right.

4 As he is nearly 180 degrees with Adam, Jean Jacques now uses his left arm to grab Adam's leg for the knee bar. Which leg he grabs depends on which foot is over the top of the other, because that is the easier leg to manipulate. In this case, Adam had his right foot over his left, so Jean Jacques grabs Adam's right leg. (Note that it would be very difficult to pull out Adam's left leg, as it is locked by his right foot.)

5 Jean Jacques falls to his left and pulls Adam's right leg, both hands on the heel, for the knee bar.

No-gi guard pass

Passing the guard in submission wrestling, or other no-gi situations, can be a very difficult proposition. You have to rely on great posture and a different set of grips to compensate for not having the gi to hold. The method demonstrated here is one of the methods preferred by top competitors because it eliminates the chance of a triangle or arm attack by the defender. It also ensures the greatest amount of control.

1 The first step in passing the guard, whether sports jiu-jitsu, submission wrestling, or even vale-tudo, is to make sure you have a proper, comfortable base to start from. If you are off balance or out of posture, any attempt to pass will result in failure or worse. In this case, you can see that Jean Jacques has proper posture, with his head up and back straight. His knees are close to Adam's hips and his right hand is on Adam's left biceps to block any attempts by Adam to raise his torso off the mat.

2 Having assured himself of the proper position to start his move, Jean Jacques's first step is to open Adam's guard. Jean Jacques places both hands on Adam's chest and pushes off, while lifting his hips. Notice that Jean Jacques places his right knee in the center of Adam's butt. He then arches back, forcing Adam to open his guard.

3 As soon as Adam opens his guard, Jean Jacques brings both arms inside and around Adam's legs, preventing any chance that Adam may have for a triangle, arm lock, or shoulder lock.

4 Jean Jacques locks his hands, closing his arms around Adam's hips. He pushes off his feet and drives his chest forward against Adam's thighs, forcing his hips off the ground. To do this move correctly, it is extremely important that you have your arms as close to your opponent's hips as possible, and your elbows closed, since the defender's best escape is to slide his hips down until he can bring one of his knees between your arms.

5 Jean Jacques pushes forward off his toes, legs straight, and drives Adam's legs over his head. He maintains close control over Adam's hips by pushing down with his chest. At this point, you must choose a side to pass. Most people prefer passing to the right, as that is the opponent's left and usually weaker side if he is right-handed. That being said, since most people pass to the right, most defenders have more practice defending their left, so they may be weaker but more skilled on that side. You should be like water; flow to whichever side shows less resistance. Since Jean Jacques decides to pass to his right, he closes his left elbow down, forcing Adam's right hip down.

6 Jean Jacques switches his hips by bringing his right knee down and reaches with his right hand until he touches the mat next to Adam's right shoulder. Again, it is very important to remain close and tight against your opponent at all times when passing the guard.

7 Jean Jacques lowers his right elbow close to Adam's right ear and lowers his torso on to Adam's chest, completing the guard pass.

No-gi attack from the back

Having the back is arguably the best position a fighter can achieve. Your opponent can't see what you are doing, which makes it easier to control him and reach submissions. The back is also a much more stable position than the mount, as your opponent can't simply bridge in his attempt to get out. Once you have reached the back, it is very important not only to keep it but also to be able to submit your opponent. You will inevitably have expended a great deal of energy to achieve the position, and if you lose it, it will not only give your opponent a boost but you may be exhausted. This technique demonstrates a surefire way to keep your opponent from escaping that combines with a choke attack to the neck.

1 Jean Jacques has Adam's back. Both hooks are in place on Adam's hips, and his head is pushing on Adam's back for tightness. Jean Jacques has his left arm under Adam's left arm, while his right one is over Adam's right shoulder as he locks his hands together.

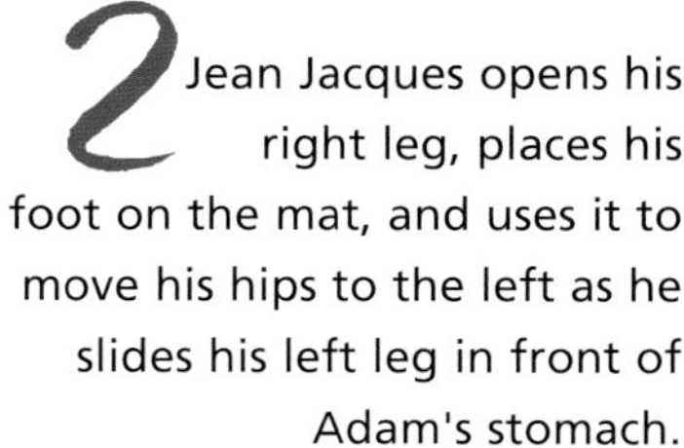

2 Jean Jacques opens his right leg, places his foot on the mat, and uses it to move his hips to the left as he slides his left leg in front of Adam's stomach.

3 Jean Jacques closes a figure-four around Adam's body, right leg locking over left foot. Almost simultaneously, now that he has secured a body lock on Adam, he release his hands, slides his right arm around Adam's neck, and locks the palms of his hands again. Notice that Jean Jacques's right arm was already over Adam's right shoulder and in front of his neck, making it a very short path to the neck.

4 Jean Jacques applies the choke by stretching his body while pulling on his right forearm with his left one.

No-gi half-guard sweep into guard pass

Although good submission wrestlers have many tools to hold off and even submit an opponent from the bottom, being on the bottom is never desirable. It's still better to be on top. And since many inferior grapplers think only one move at a time, you can often gain an advantage by not just settling for an escape but instantly transitioning to an attack, as Jean Jacques does here. His opponent is in his half guard and is attempting to pass. Jean Jacques will use the space created by his opponent's passing technique to create a sweep and immediately follow it right to the guard pass.

1 Jean Jacques has Adam in his half guard, trapping Adam's left leg by placing his left leg over Adam's calf, locked by his right foot. Notice Adam has his arms locked around Jean Jacques's head and right arm.

2 Adam starts his attempt to pass the half guard by planting his left hand on the mat, lifting his hips, and pushing his torso forward on Jean Jacques's chest. His first objective is to free his left knee from Jean Jacques's legs and then slide it to either side of Jean Jacques's hips to pass. Sensing this, Jean Jacques traps Adam's foot with his left foot now, and switches his hips to his left. He also uses his left hand to push and block Adam's hips.

3 In one movement, Jean Jacques wraps his left hand inside Adam's right leg and slides his left knee between their hips until it is near the left ribs, locking his right foot on the outside of Adam's left foot to prevent him from moving. Jean Jacques uses his left arm to help pull himself under Adam's body. This is the key for most half-guard sweeps, as you must be underneath the opponent for them to work. At this point, the direction of the sweep will be determined by Adam's reaction. If he were to brace forward and plant both his arms on the mat, Jean Jacques would simply slide through Adam's legs and end up on Adam's back, with Adam on all fours. In this case, however, Adam chooses to balance on top of Jean Jacques, so the sweep is to Jean Jacques's left.

4 Jean Jacques releases his right foot from Adam's foot, opens his left leg as he kicks his foot up, and turns his body left and into Adam, causing Adam to fall back.

5 As he completes the sweep, Jean Jacques immediately follows up by slipping on top of Adam and preparing for the guard pass by wrapping his arms around Adam's legs, as he did in the pass shown in position 92.

6 Once he has his arms locked in place, Jean Jacques pushes forward with his body onto Adam's legs, causing Adam to turn on his back.

7 Continuing with the guard pass explained in position 92, this time Jean Jacques passes to his left.

No-gi half-guard sweep: opponent braces forward

Position 94 demonstrated a half-guard sweep into a guard pass. In that case, the opponent reacted to Jean Jacques's action by trying to balance his weight over Jean Jacques. This position takes up with position 94, step 3. As in that case, the direction of the sweep is determined by the opponent's reaction. This time, he braces forward, throwing all his weight forward as well, making it very difficult for Jean Jacques to sweep him to his left. Jean Jacques is left with two choices: he could slip through his opponent's legs and take the back, or use this variation, in which he changes his motion, sweeps his opponent forward, and passes the guard. Because slipping through the legs would give his opponent more of a chance to roll forward and replace the guard, or simply stand up and avoid contact, Jean Jacques prefers to apply the sweep and not only score points but also have his opponent on the bottom and under control.

1 Jean Jacques has Adam in his half guard and is attempting the sweep shown in position 94. This time, however, Adam defends by throwing his weight forward.

2 Jean Jacques starts a technical stand-up position, bracing off his right arm and raising his torso while pulling his right leg through.

3 Since he still has control of Adam's right leg with his left arm, Jean Jacques continues to stand up, causing Adam to fall to his side.

4 As soon as Adam's back hits the mat, Jean Jacques starts his guard pass. He reaches with his right hand and controls Adam's left knee so he can't replace the guard, while still controlling Adam's right leg with his left arm.

5 Jean Jacques braces his right hand on the ground and throws his left leg back, clearing Adam's left leg.

6 Jean Jacques completes the guard pass by positioning his left knee close to Adam's left hip, right hand around Adam's head and shoulder pressing against Adam's chin to flatten him out.

No-gi half guard to Omoplata

In this technique, Jean Jacques takes advantage of the half guard and goes directly for an Omoplata, or shoulder lock, submission. The arm position—Jean Jacques locking the opponent's left arm—happens quite frequently when an opponent attempts to pass by wrapping the arm and crossing the knee. Jean Jacques counters it by blocking with his right knee and locking the arm back with his right arm.

1 Jean Jacques has Adam in his half guard. Adam is attempting to pass the half guard by wrapping his left arm under Jean Jacques's right arm, switching his hip and crossing his knee. Jean Jacques has already turned sideways to defend this, and blocks the pass by placing his right knee in front of Adam's hips. He then wraps his own right arm back around Adam's left arm.

2 With a sudden move, Jean Jacques opens his right leg, releasing the block on Adam's hips and causing him to fall forward. Jean Jacques encourages that by leaning back and pulling Adam with him by the left arm. Notice that he still has his left leg trapping Adam's left calf, so Adam can't pass the guard.

3 Jean Jacques continues to lean back, straightening Adam's left arm as he goes back, and throws his right leg over Adam's head.

4 Jean Jacques locks his foot in front of Adam's face and slides his right hand from Adam's elbow to his hand.

5 Jean Jacques continues to sit forward for the Omoplata.

No-gi half-guard sweep using the opponent's leg

This position starts much like the other half-guard sweeps and attacks. Again the opponent is attempting to pass the guard by sliding his arm inside Jean Jacques's arm. He has his arm wrapped under Jean Jacques's arm and will attempt to escape the knee and cross it over to escape the leg. If Jean Jacques doesn't react, his guard will most likely be passed.

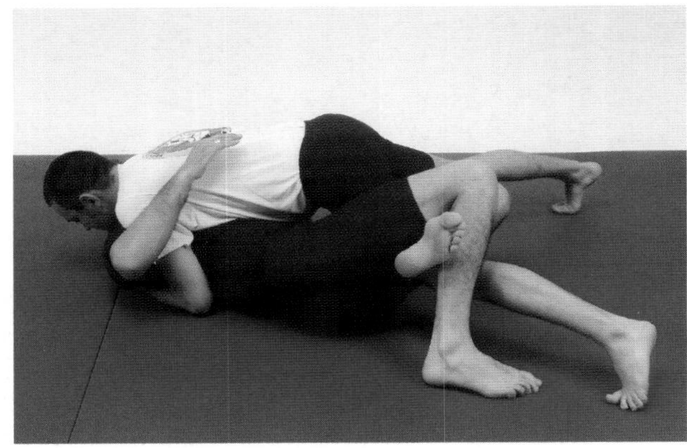

1 Adam is attempting to escape and pass the half guard. He has his left arm wrapped around Jean Jacques right arm and is lifting his hips to free his left knee from the grip of Jean Jacques's legs.

2 Jean Jacques's first step is to turn sideways and slide his right arm inside and around Adam's arm. Once he has his arm freed from Adam's grasp, he can proceed with a variety of escapes and sweeps.

3 Jean Jacques "shrimps" (brings his head to Adam's hips) and grabs Adam's left leg with his right hand. Notice that this entire time, Jean Jacques hasn't released his left-foot trap of Adam's left leg, otherwise Adam would be free to pass the guard.

4 Jean Jacques continues to tuck his upper body into Adam, using his right foot to hook under Adam's left foot and lift it until he can grab it with his right hand as well.

5 Jean Jacques rolls back over to his right as he opens his right leg and pulls with his right arm on Adam's left leg, bringing Adam with him. Notice that there is a lot of outward pressure on Adam's left knee, so Adam is forced to follow the sweep as well to prevent damage to his knee.

6 Jean Jacques continues to roll to his right. Once Adam begins to fall over, he switches, grabs Adam's legs with both hands, and goes up on his toes, completing the sweep.

No-gi across-side to mount to head-and-arm choke

The head-and-arm choke is a great submission position that can be used with equal effectiveness in both sports jiu-jitsu and submission wrestling. Position 87 demonstrated one way to achieve the head-and-arm choke when your opponent has his forearm in front of your throat to create space. In this variation, the opponent's arm is in a more difficult spot, so Jean Jacques will feign that he is going for the mount, then switch to the head-and-arm choke. This technique can be used to achieve the coveted mount position as well.

1 Jean Jacques is across-side on Adam. Notice that Adam's right arm is behind Jean Jacques's back and Jean Jacques has his hips switched and is preparing for the mount. His right elbow is locked into Adam's right armpit and he has his back to Adam to block Adam's view of what is happening. Simultaneously, he uses his left hand to push Adam's knees to the left, so he can mount by throwing his left leg over.

2 Jean Jacques switches his hips back and brings in his right arm until he places his hand near Adam's left ear. This action forces Adam's arm across his face.

3 Jean Jacques wraps his right arm around Adam's head, locking Adam's arm in position in front of his neck. It is very important for Jean Jacques to keep his chest close to Adam's chest at all times so Adam doesn't have any space to remove his right arm.

4 Jean Jacques braces off his left hand as he slides his left knee across Adam's stomach to achieve the mount. He also pushes forward with his chest, adding pressure on Adam's neck.

5 Once he mounts on Adam, Jean Jacques closes his arms by locking his right hand onto his left biceps, placing his left hand on Adam's head, and applies the choking pressure by pressing forward with his chest against Adam's arm as he brings his elbows together.

No-gi across-side to two arm locks

The beauty of this technique is that it takes a difficult position to advance from and demonstrates how to do a submission on either arm, which keeps your opponent guessing until it is too late.

1 Jean Jacques is across-side on Bryce and Bryce locks his arms around him and holds him tight.

2 Pushing off his toes, Jean Jacques pushes forward with his torso, switches his hips, and steps across with his left foot.

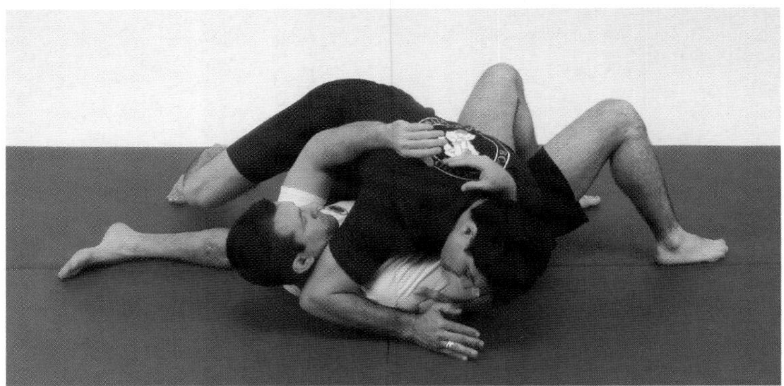

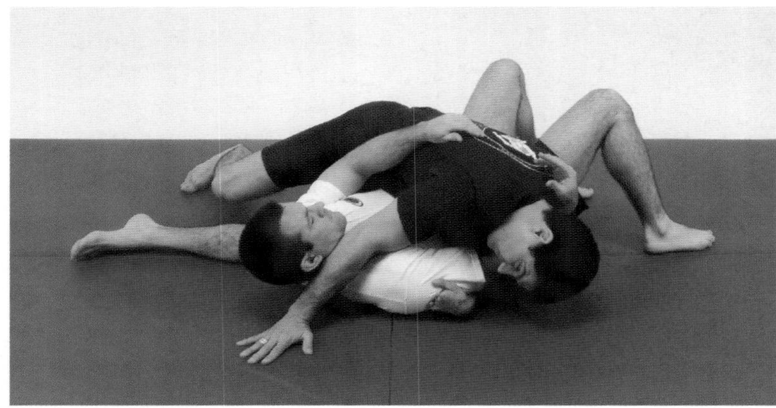

3 He then places his right hand on the mat so that his right arm blocks Bryce's head. He continues to push forward with his torso, breaking Bryce's grip.

4 Jean Jacques steps over Bryce's head with his right leg, locks Bryce’s wrist between his head and left shoulder, and clasps his hands together so that his left forearm is directly behind Bryce's right elbow.

5 Jean Jacques pushes his head further forward and down toward the mat, while at the same time he pulls his forearm up, causing pressure on Bryce's elbow for the arm lock.

6 Alternatively, he can lock Bryce's left wrist under his right armpit and apply an arm lock to the left arm by simply pushing his hips forward.

The Twister

Many of your prime opportunities in submission wrestling come not when your opponent is defending himself but when he takes a stab at escaping. By their nature, escapes leave one vulnerable. "The Twister" is a wrestling position called the guillotine adapted to submission wrestling. While the regular guillotine is mostly a neck crank, this version can be used for a variety of submissions. In this technique, the opponent has turned into Jean Jacques to escape the across-side position, and Jean Jacques hooks his leg and creates several submissions from there. The secret of this position is to be able to spin your body under the opponent as you roll him over.

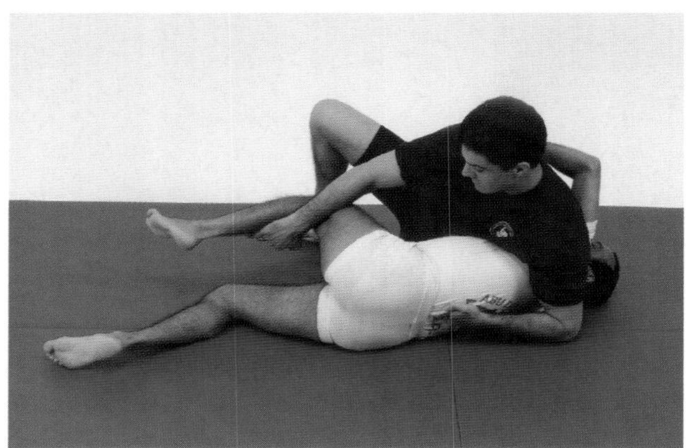

1 Kid turns into Jean Jacques, trying to escape the across-side. Jean Jacques hooks Kid's left leg at the calf with his right arm.

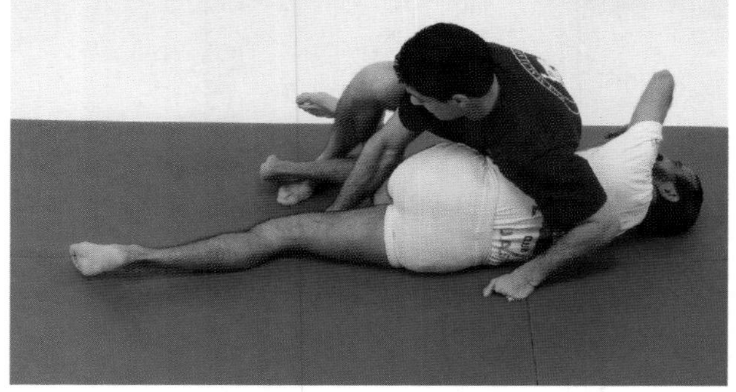

2 Jean Jacques slides his left leg and wraps it over Kid's left leg. Jean Jacques then closes a figure-four around it by looping his own right leg over his left foot.

3 Jean Jacques grabs Kid's right leg with both arms and rolls over his own left shoulder, bringing Kid with him by the legs. Notice the figure-four around Kid's left leg.

4 As he brings Kid over with him, Jean Jacques pulls himself by the arms, spins his own body under himself, and ends up with his head on the opposite side of where he started. He then grabs Kid's right arm with both arms, preventing him from turning over, and submits him with a wishbone. The wishbone should be your first choice as it is the first available submission. Many of today's fighters, however, are so flexible that they will not submit to it, so following are three other submissions that give you a variety of surprises to spring on your unsuspecting victim.

5 As an alternative, Jean Jacques reaches around Kid's head with both hands and pulls it toward himself for the neck-crank submission.

6 Or he may choose to pull Kid over his torso and reach for the rear-naked choke.

7 Another option: Jean Jacques wraps Kid's right arm for a Kimura lock.

No-gi butterfly guard sweep

One of the main differences in the butterfly guard when not having a gi to hold on to is that you need to lock your hands underneath your opponent's arms. When you have the gi, you can grab his sleeves or collar to control him, but without it you should resort to having your arms inside and under his arms. Another important piece of a successful butterfly guard sweep is that you must sit up, with your back off the mat and your hips away from your opponent, to be able to rock back and forth. From there, you can sweep your opponent, take his back, or even attack his leg for a knee bar.

1 Jean Jacques has Bryce in the butterfly guard. He is in great position, with his back off the ground, hips back from Bryce, and his arms under Bryce's arms, locked around the back.

2 Jean Jacques sits back and pulls Bryce's torso with him as he opens his feet, spreading Bryce's legs.

3 Jean Jacques puts his right foot on the mat, switches his body to his right, and lassoes Bryce's left leg with his right arm while his left hand grips Bryce's right elbow.

4 Pushing off his right leg, Jean Jacques starts to rise for the reversal. He pulls Bryce's right arm with his left hand as he lifts his left leg. Notice that Jean Jacques maintains his left foot hooked on Bryce's right leg, so Bryce can't slide it open and block Jean Jacques from coming over him.

5 Jean Jacques continues to come over the top of Bryce and completes the reversal.

No-gi butterfly guard sweep to foot lock

This sweep can be used successfully with or without the gi. When you spring it, often your opponent will brace with one of his arms and try to sit back up, and then you and he are in a stalemate. Perfect time to go for a foot lock and end the match right there. Another good time for the foot lock is right as your opponent falls back. He will be surprised and concentrating on reestablishing his position, and probably not thinking about defending a submission.

1 Kid is attempting to pass the guard standing up. He is controlling Jean Jacques's knees with his hands and will perhaps try to push them to the side or down to complete the pass. Jean Jacques has his hooks inside Kid's legs and is holding Kid's wrist with his hands.

2 Jean Jacques quickly drops his hands and grabs Kid's ankles as he kicks his shins up behind Kid's knees, lifting him off the mat.

3 Jean Jacques continues and pulls on Kid's ankles for the sweep.

4 As Kid is about to hit the mat with his back, Jean Jacques kicks his left leg straight and wraps it around Kid's right leg, placing his foot on Kid's hips, while he maintains his right knee between Kid's legs. At the same time, Jean Jacques has wrapped his left arm around Kid's left foot for the foot lock.

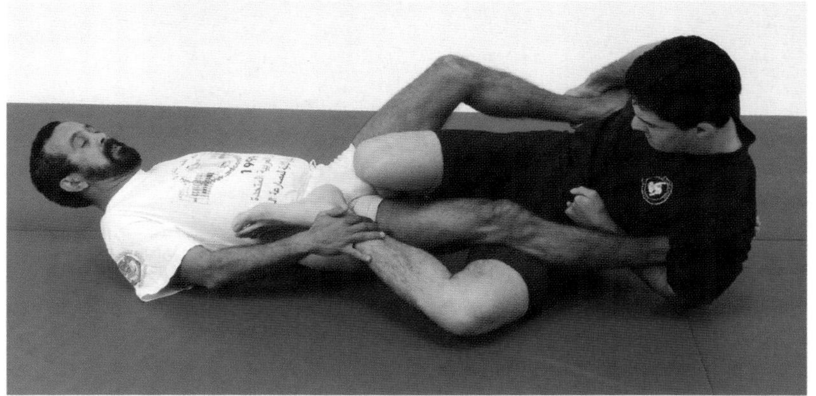

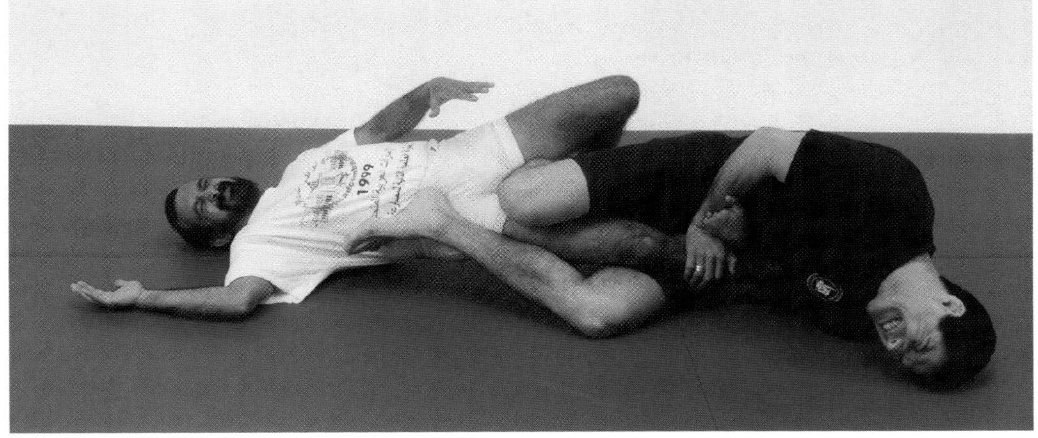

5 Jean Jacques applies the pressure by locking his right hand onto his left wrist and stretching his torso, twisting Kid's foot.

No-gi butterfly guard sweep to knee bar

In this technique, Jean Jacques uses a variation of the previous sweep and attacks his opponent's leg, rather than the foot. The straight foot lock from the previous position should be your first option, as going for the knee bar puts you in a difficult position if your opponent manages to escape from it and get behind you near your back. However, the foot lock is difficult against someone with legs longer than yours. The knee bar works better in such a case, since those long legs provide you with even greater leverage.

1 Jean Jacques has Kid in his guard with hooks. This time, however, Jean Jacques switches both legs to one side, in order to have greater leverage to sweep his opponent to that side. By using the power of both legs against one side, Jean Jacques will force Kid to fall back to that side. Jean Jacques has both shins on Kid's left thigh and is holding Kid's left ankle with his right hand, while his left hand controls Kid's right wrist.

2 Jean Jacques pulls Kid's left ankle as he extends his legs, causing Kid to fall back.

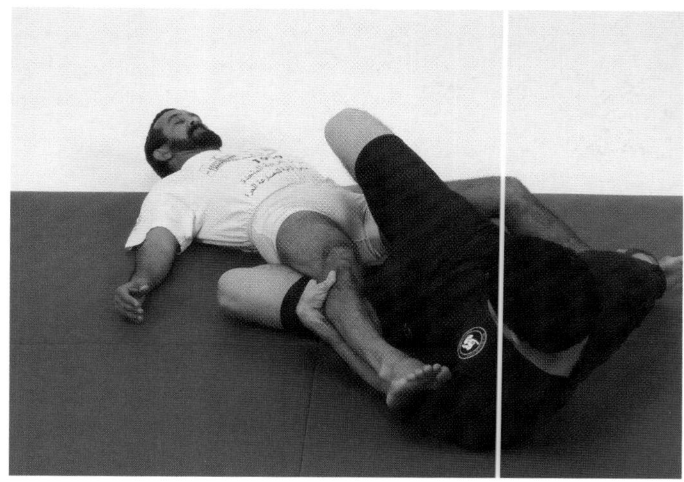

3 Jean Jacques wraps his left arm behind Kid's right ankle and pulls it toward his head as he slides his own left knee under Kid's right leg. Note that Jean Jacques is still holding Kid's left ankle to make sure Kid doesn't pop back up.

4 Jean Jacques spins his body over Kid's by throwing his right leg over Kid's right leg and pulling it up.

5 Once in control of Kid's leg, Jean Jacques extends his torso and pulls the leg with both arms across his hips for the knee bar.

No-gi open-guard submission heel hook and foot-lock variation

Generally, taking the gi off makes it more difficult for a better fighter to submit a lesser fighter. The slipperiness makes submissions tough to stick. However, Jean Jacques's arsenal of connected and dangerous techniques has given him uncanny success with no-gi submissions. This position shows off a pair of his classic attacks from the open guard.

1 Jean Jacques has Kid in his open guard. His right foot is hooked on Kid's leg, his right hand holding Kid's left ankle, while he controls Kid's right wrist with his left hand and keeps distance with his left foot on Kid's hip.

2 To start the attack, Jean Jacques pushes Kid's right knee with his left leg, causing Kid to lean to his right. Jean Jacques then slides his right leg between Kid's legs and begins to loop it over his left leg, simultaneously slipping his right arm around Kid's left foot. Kid has pivoted on his toes to keep balance. If Jean Jacques plans to go for a foot lock instead of the heel hook, he will wrap his arm around Kid's ankle instead of the foot. Note that heels hooks are illegal in some competitions because of the damage they can cause to the knee joint.

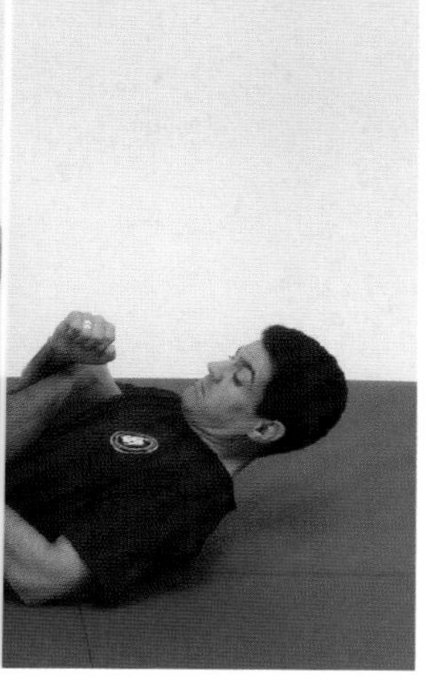

3 Jean Jacques pushes Kid's right knee with his left leg, forcing the knee down as he hooks Kid's left ankle in the crease of his right arm and locks Kid's toes under his armpit.

4 With Kid face-down on the mat, Jean Jacques's right leg is over Kid's torso, keeping him from spinning, and Jean Jacques's heel hook is set in place. Jean Jacques applies torque to the heel by twisting his torso to the left. Notice that the heel hook applies pressure to the knee joint as well as the heel.

5 In this option, Jean Jacques applies a foot lock by turning to his knees and arching his torso back while holding Kid's foot.

No-gi open-guard pass to both sides

Passing the guard is daunting enough with the gi, but it becomes a nightmare without it. A defender with a good guard will be able to slip away and keep distance from you, taking away perhaps the two most important factors in passing someone's guard: the ability to control hip movement and put your body on the defender. In most cases you have to work to control one side and prevent the defender from opening up any space to free his knees and use them to block you. In this case, Jean Jacques uses a clever technique to control both legs at once and prevent his opponent from using them to create space. Notice that Jean Jacques controls the legs and puts them to one side. When faced with resistance from the opponent, he will simply change the direction of the pass, rather than fight through the block. This is one of the most important lessons you can have in technique use in general: don't fight power with power, simply go around it.

1 Jean Jacques is attempting to pass Kid's open guard. At this point they are not in contact with each other.

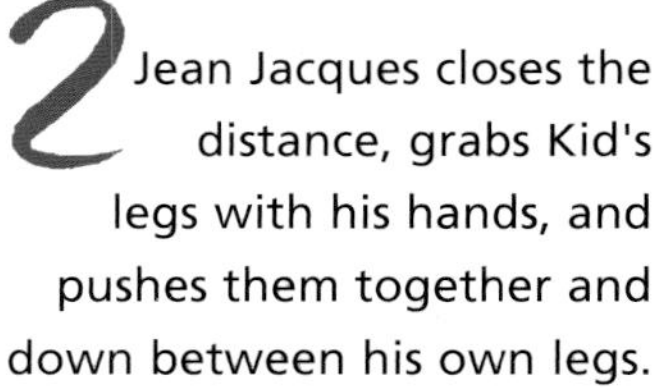

2 Jean Jacques closes the distance, grabs Kid's legs with his hands, and pushes them together and down between his own legs.

3 Jean Jacques closes his legs, trapping Kid's feet, and kneels on the ground. He wraps his right arm under Kid's knees, making sure his hand clasps Kid's far calf.

4 Jean Jacques turns his torso to the left, deflects Kid's knees with his right shoulder, and puts his weight on Kid's legs with his chest. Kid starts to defend with both arms, ready to push Jean Jacques's head to create the space needed to free his hips.

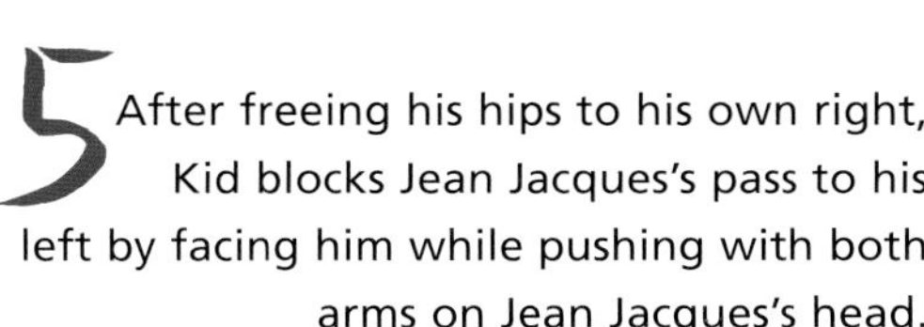

5 After freeing his hips to his own right, Kid blocks Jean Jacques's pass to his left by facing him while pushing with both arms on Jean Jacques's head.

6 Pushing off his right leg, Jean Jacques immediately pivots his body to his right. That will force his left shoulder down, deflecting Kid's knees. Again he puts his chest on Kid's hips to control the pass, but this time he is further up on Kid's body, making it more difficult for Kid to find the space to push and free his hips.

No-gi guard pass to arm lock

In this technique, Jean Jacques goes for the traditional under-the-leg guard pass, but has his progress impeded by the opponent's arm blocking his hips. However, as so often in jiu-jitsu, a difficulty and an opportunity are two sides of the same coin: the arm may impede the guard pass, but it also serves up an arm lock to the alert practitioner.

1 Jean Jacques is on his knees, passing Kid's guard under the leg. His left hand pushes down on Kid's right knee. Kid's left leg rests on Jean Jacques's right shoulder as Jean Jacques wraps his arm around it.

2 Jean Jacques pushes off his legs and drives forward onto Kid, locking his head and right arm around Kid's left leg.

3 Jean Jacques drives his right fist to the mat to create the leverage to pivot around Kid's leg for the guard pass. At this point, Kid blocks the pass with his left hand on Jean Jacques's right hip and his right arm on Jean Jacques's right elbow. Notice that Jean Jacques still has his left hand pressing down on Kid's right knee, to keep control of that side and to prevent Kid from putting that foot down and pushing to free his hips to the right, from where he could face Jean Jacques and throw a right leg in front of Jean Jacques's face to block his pass.

4 Jean Jacques lets go of Kid's left knee as he plants his left hand on the mat and switches his hips, deflecting Kid's power. Jean Jacques slides his left knee over Kid's stomach and begins to sit back.

5 Jean Jacques swings his right arm around, locking Kid's left arm, passes his right leg over Kid's head, and falls back for the arm lock.

No-gi guard pass: opponent blocks

As in position 106, Jean Jacques goes for the traditional under-the-leg guard pass, but has his progress impeded by his opponent's arm blocking his hips. Unlike position 106, however, this time the opponent is using both arms to block Jean Jacques's pass, rather than just one. Jean Jacques could still use the previous technique and attempt the arm lock, but that gives the opponent a chance to escape and reverse the position. This time, Jean Jacques prefers to secure the guard pass, rather than go for the riskier submission. Although that is not his general style, there are moments in competition when all you need is a few points and it would be foolish to risk going for a submission.

1 Jean Jacques is passing the guard to his right and Kid starts to block, both arms straight on Jean Jacques's shoulder. As Jean Jacques continues to pass, Kid pushes Jean Jacques's body with his arms straight.

2 As Jean Jacques continues to pass, Kid changes strategy and puts both arms straight on Jean Jacques's torso in an attempt to block the pass. Jean Jacques puts his right fist on the mat and raises his hips, deflecting Kid's power by changing the angle of his arms (now they are pushing up instead of forward).

3 With Kid's block nullified, Jean Jacques continues to circle over Kid's head. Notice that as Jean Jacques continues to circle around, he causes Kid's arms to actually rise and twist over Kid.

4 Jean Jacques finishes the pass by reaching the left side of Kid and puts his weight down on top of Kid's crossed arms.

No-gi open-guard pass to knee bar

Passing the guard in most cases involves controlling the distance between you and the defender, controlling his hips or legs, and applying your body weight to his body to prevent movement. With the gi to grab, you have more control of the defender. Without the gi, the defender gets a lot more slippery, especially when he sweats. If he has good leg and hip movement, he can block your attempts and keep creating distance between you and him. If you are a submissions specialist like Jean Jacques, however, the secret is to not get too focused on the pass, because one of the pitfalls of the open guard is that the defender exposes his feet and legs to submission holds. In this case, Jean Jacques opts to forget the pass and go directly to a knee bar.

1 Jean Jacques is attempting to pass Kid's open guard. His left knee pushes down and blocks Kid's right leg as his right arm hooks Kid's left leg to pass under it. Kid readies his left hand to block Jean Jacques's right knee and defend the pass.

2 Jean Jacques twists his body to his right as he slides his left knee across, until he kneels down on the mat next to Kid's left hip. Notice that Jean Jacques is hooking Kid's left leg at the bend of his right arm, trapping it as if in a vise while keeping both his hands free.

3 Jean Jacques continues to turn his body to his right, letting his left leg trap Kid's leg, and slides his right arm along Kid's leg as he pulls it up. Jean Jacques drops his back to the mat as he pulls Kid's left foot across his hips with both hands for the knee bar.

No-gi open-guard pass to foot lock

In the previous position, Jean Jacques short-circuited the open guard and took advantage of one of its weaknesses by attacking with a knee bar. In this case, he opts for an even more immediate attack as he simply goes for the foot lock. One advantage of the foot lock is that, if it fails, you haven't given up your back to the opponent, as you do in the knee bar. However, foot locks can be tough to land against people who have great flexibility or much longer legs than you. Your opponent's physical characteristics will help you determine your approach.

1 Jean Jacques is attempting to pass the open guard. He pushes down with his left leg and hand on Kid's right leg to block it or pass over it. Kid holds Jean Jacques's left ankle with his right hand and keeps pushing Jean Jacques's hips with his left leg to create space, making it difficult for Jean Jacques to pass.

2 Jean Jacques wraps his right arm around Kid's left foot, trapping it under his armpit, and begins to lean back. Notice that he keeps pressing his hand and knee on Kid's right leg.

3 As he starts to lower himself to the mat, Jean Jacques hooks his left foot on the outside of Kid's left hip, putting his chin behind Kid's left knee. This locks Kid's leg in place.

4 Jean Jacques lowers his body to the mat, places his right foot on Kid's left armpit to prevent him from popping up and defending the foot lock, and applies pressure to Kid's left foot by arching his torso, causing Kid's foot to bend back.

No-gi open-guard hook pass to leg lock

In this variation of the open-guard pass, the opponent hooks his left foot around Jean Jacques's right leg to attempt a sweep or to maintain some distance. This is commonly known as the De La Riva guard. Jean Jacques once again cleverly uses the position's weakness to his benefit as he applies a leg lock.

1 Jean Jacques is attempting to pass Kid's De La Riva guard. Jean Jacques has his left hand on Kid's right knee and his right one on Kid's left knee.

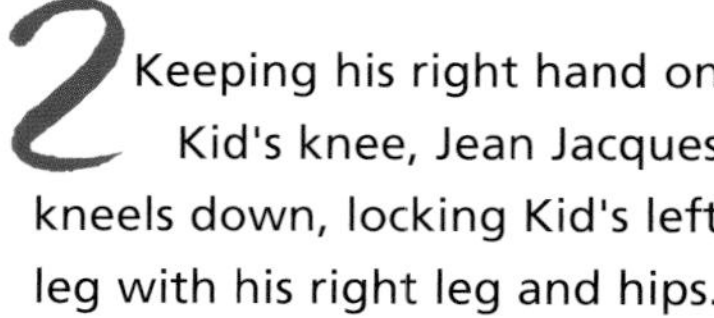

2 Keeping his right hand on Kid's knee, Jean Jacques kneels down, locking Kid's left leg with his right leg and hips.

3 Jean Jacques rolls over his right shoulder while still controlling Kid's left leg with his right hand and leg.

4 As he rolls, Jean Jacques brings Kid with him.

5 Jean Jacques locks his legs in a figure-four by throwing his left leg over his right foot while rolling. As he lands, he wraps his arms around Kid's left thigh and pulls them toward himself, applying pressure on Kid's quadriceps.

No-gi butterfly guard pass

Being able to pass the butterfly guard is essential to black belt fighting, because it is a very common guard used by many top fighters. If you have trouble passing it, this will become known and your opponents will use it again and again. Notice that here Jean Jacques's opponent has both feet inside Jean Jacques's legs and his back on the mat. From this position, he has many options: he can sit up for a sweep, or pull one of Jean Jacques's arms across and slip to his back. The first thing in Jean Jacques's mind is to neutralize the hooks and block his opponent's ability to extend his legs. He does this by locking his elbows to his knees, eliminating the power of the butterfly guard.

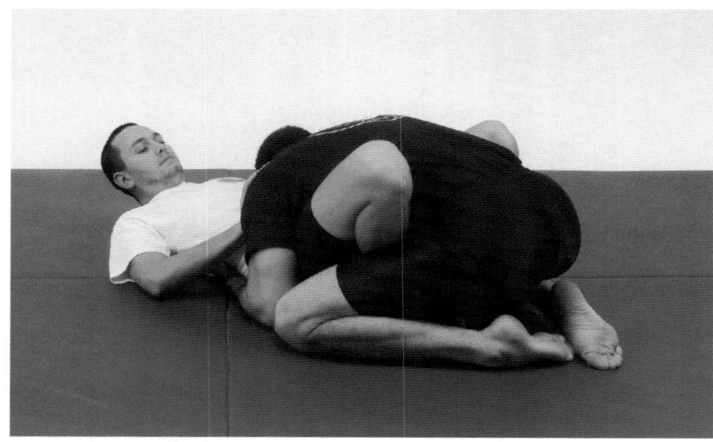

1 Jean Jacques attempts to pass Adam's guard with hooks. He locks his elbows to his knees, blocking Adam's legs in place.

2 Jean Jacques transfers his hands from Adam's back to Adam's ankles and lifts his hips off his toes. Notice that Jean Jacques is pressing his head on Adam's stomach to keep him from moving.

3 Jean Jacques decides to pass to his left, so he pivots off his left foot, lowers his left hip, and throws his right leg over and around Adam's legs. Adam cannot follow Jean Jacques's leg with his left hook because of Jean Jacques's grip on both of his feet.

4 Jean Jacques brings his right knee next to Adam's right knee, pushing against the V of the leg. He then releases his hands from Adam's ankles as he slides his right knee to the ground. He completes the pass by adjusting his left knee out and placing his left arm on the opposite side of Adam's body. It is very important to bring your right knee close to your opponent's right leg, otherwise he may replace the guard.

No-gi half-guard pass to knee bar

This technique demonstrates another quick submission from a guard pass. The half guard can be very difficult to pass in no-gi fighting, especially if your opponent has strong legs and decides to keep them locked. The trick to open the lock is to grab behind your opponent's butt and lock your arms tightly around his legs. As you stretch your body back, you will force his legs open, as you are using the power of your entire body against his crossed ankles. From there, it is a simple matter to switch to the submission.

1 Jean Jacques is in Kid's half guard and Kid has locked his legs and refuses to open, making it very difficult for Jean Jacques to pass.

2 Jean Jacques places his hands on Kid's chest and pushes off, sliding his torso back away from Kid's head.